THEO ANGELOPOULOS
INTERVIEWS

CONVERSATIONS WITH FILMMAKERS SERIES
PETER BRUNETTE, GENERAL EDITOR

Courtesy of Photofest

THEO ANGELOPOULOS
INTERVIEWS
EDITED BY DAN FAINARU

UNIVERSITY PRESS OF MISSISSIPPI / JACKSON

www.upress.state.ms.us

Copyright © 2001 by University Press of Mississippi
All rights reserved
Manufactured in the United States of America

∞

Library of Congress Cataloging-in-Publication Data

Angelopoulos, Theodoros, 1935–
    Theo Angelopoulos : interviews / edited by Dan Fainaru.
      p. cm.—(Conversations with filmmakers series)
    Filmography: p.
    Includes index.
    ISBN 1-57806-215-2 (cloth : alk. paper)—ISBN 1-57806-216-0 (pbk. : alk. paper)
    1. Angelopoulos, Thodåros, 1935–   Interviews. 2. Motion picture producers and directors—Greece—Interviews.   I. Fainaru, Dan. II. Title. III. Series.

PN1998.3.A53 A5 2001
791.43'0233'092—dc21   00-043515

British Library Cataloging-in-Publication Data available

CONTENTS

Introduction   vii

Chronology   xix

Filmography   xxiii

An Elegy for a Land Rotting Away: Reconstruction   3
    FLORIAN HOPF

Unveiling the Patterns of Power: *The Days of '36*   9
    ULRICH GREGOR

A Journey through Greek Landscape and History: *The Travelling Players*   16
    MICHEL DEMOPOULOS AND FRIDA LIAPPAS

Rhythms of Silence to Better Underline the Scream: *The Hunters*   23
    FRANCESCO CASETTI

Animating Dead Space and Dead Time: *Megalexandros*   28
    TONY MITCHELL

The Growing of Tomatoes   33
    GIDEON BACHMANN

A Withered Apple: *Voyage to Cythera*   39
    MICHEL GRODENT

Talking about *The Beekeeper*   53
    MICHEL CIMENT

Landscape in the Mist   60
SERGE TOUBIANA AND FRÉDÉRIC STRAUSS

Angelopoulos's Philosophy of Film   66
GERALD O'GRADY

Silence Is as Meaningful as Any Dialogue: *The Suspended Step of the Stork*   75
EDNA FAINARU

National Culture and Individual Vision   83
ANDREW HORTON

Homer's Where the Heart Is: *Ulysses' Gaze*   89
GEOFF ANDREW

The Human Experience in One Gaze: *Ulysses' Gaze*   93
DAN FAINARU

The Time That Flows By: *Eternity and a Day*   101
GIDEON BACHMANN

The Time of His Life: *Eternity and a Day*   113
GEOFF ANDREW

I Shoot the Way I Breathe: *Eternity and a Day*   117
GABRIELLE SCHULZ

. . . And about All the Rest   123
DAN FAINARU

Index   151

INTRODUCTION

THEO ANGELOPOULOS MAY NOT be a household name, certainly not in America, but there are very few, if any, filmmakers in the history of cinema who qualify better for the classic definition of *film auteur.* Every shot in every sequence of every film he has made bears his indelible artistic personality. A unique thematic pattern transcends his entire work. A short glance at any of the pictures he directed, at any point—beginning, middle, or end—is sufficient to reveal the identity of the author behind them. You may love his kind of cinema, admire it, and be fascinated by it, as many of us do. You may hate it, be annoyed by it, and find it boring, and there are as many—if not more—who feel that way about him. But whatever your opinion of his work, you have to concede the presence of a distinct, determined, and precise guiding concept behind it all, both in form and content. While Angelopoulos remains a somewhat solitary figure in the world of film, his is one of the most significant voices in modern cinema.

Born in Athens, Greece, in 1935, Theo Angelopoulos was a World War II child, growing up in a country constantly shaken by political turmoil, dictatorships, and civil wars which started before the war and went on long after it was officially finished. Many of these memories would eventually find their way into his films, particularly the disappearance of his father, arrested one day for no obvious reason, deported, and almost given up for dead before he returned home as suddenly as he had vanished. To fulfill the expectations of his middle class family, Angelopoulos dutifully entered the Athens Law School, but four years later, on the eve of graduation, he packed his suitcase and left for Paris to study cinema. After one rebellious year at the famed IDHEC film school, he moved to the Musée de l'Homme to study with film ethnographer Jean Rouch, working at night as an usher at the French Cinematheque to support himself. A product of the idealistic sixties, he absorbed much of the insurgent spirit of the Paris student population, pre-1968. At the time, the radical left seemed to carry with it all the promises of a brave and better new world to come, once it defeated the old conservative spirit, and the duty of all good people was to struggle for its victory. The turmoil he found in Greece when he returned home only encouraged him to persist in this belief and to apply it to his own country. For a while, he wrote film reviews for a left-wing magazine, *Democratic Change,* until it was closed down by the regime. After one failed attempt to complete a first film, *Forminx Story,* and a short radio show satire, *The Broadcast,* he finally embarked in 1970 with a group of friends and no money to speak of on his first feature film, *Reconstruction.*

In a booklet published by the Greek Film Center for a 1998 London retrospective of his films, Angelopoulos, who divides his career into three distinct periods, describes the first as a time of "historical, political films which coincides with a more general ideological turmoil in Western Europe." Talking to the late German film critic Florian Hopf specifically about *Reconstruction,* he says that for him, "the film . . . is an elegy for a land rotting away, abandoned by its inhabitants. It all started in 1962 when West German subsidies included the permission for Greek citizens to live and work in Germany. This issue was hotly debated at the time by both the right-wing and left-wing papers in Greece. Some claimed emigration is nothing less than a disaster; others believed it was rather positive, for if many workers went away, there would be no danger of an organized working class and therefore no resistance to the regime in power. The Colonels prefer, these days, to see all their opponents leave the country. All my friends, for instance, live abroad . . . unless they are in prison. It is for them that I made *Reconstruction.*"

Censorship was a major issue at the time; avoiding a direct confrontation with it, a major worry. In 1973, when *The Days of '36* was screened by the Berlin Forum, Angelopoulos remarked to Ulrich Gregor, "To tell you the truth, there is quite a bit of difference between the original script and the film, in its final form." He did not go much more into detail, for obvious reasons. However, to clarify the modern context of the film, he pointed out that "our present political situation is not unlike the time when the King intervened in favor of [pre–World War II dictator General] Metaxas, after realizing the two leading parties were unable to reach an agreement on their own." He is proud to mention the film was made with the help of a rich acquaintance, who told him after the film: "I don't care if I lose money on your film. The experience was worth it, through this film I learned a lot of things I did not know before." Unveiling historical truths for the eyes of the innocent is the role of political films, as far Angelopoulos is concerned.

The culminating point of that first period was *The Travelling Players*, the perfect symbiosis of cinema art, innovative film language, history, politics, and elliptical statements. After its Cannes screening in a sidebar section, "The Directors' Fortnight," Angelopoulos's international reputation was firmly established. The next time he visited Cannes, with *The Hunters*, he was already in the official competition, recognized as one of the new masters of the medium.

All through that period, the Brechtian influence, which has been an integral part of his personal vision since his stay in Paris, was pronounced in each of the films he made. Talking with Francesco Casetti about a specific shot in *The Hunters*, he explains: "The . . . scene you mention is a long sequence shot showing two people making love, a group sitting around the table eating, the American woman walking in and offering to buy everything, the politician undressing. By moving from one to the other in one sweeping camera movement, we reveal the many facets of one central situation and at the same time prevent the viewer from identifying with any of these facets, since he is jolted from one surprise to another. This way, we multiply one aspect while canceling another. This is what Brecht meant by alienation."

As time passed and the political conditions in his own country and all over Europe changed, clear-cut notions of good vs. bad, right vs. wrong and particularly right vs. left, were invaded by vast areas of gray. Angelopoulos came to accept the fact that power corrupts not only on the right but on the left too. He made *Megalexandros*, he tells *Sight and Sound* in 1980, to show the danger threatening the transformation of any authority or power, regardless of how noble were its initial intentions, into despotism. Since that time, he implies again and again in many of his interviews that politics has become a cynical game and has turned its back on the commitments of the past. "For a very long time we used to dream that politics was not a profession; it was a creed, a faith, an ideal. But in recent years, I have become convinced politics is nothing more than just another profession, that's all," he tells Edna Fainaru in 1991, after the screening of *The Suspended Step of the Stork*.

After completing *Megalexandros* Angelopoulos began to sense that his own role as an artist was about to change as well. Talking in 1985 about *Voyage to Cythera* to Belgian critic Michel Grodent, he argues that the film is intended to "offer the Greek audience a possibility to face the future without the traumas of the past." His disenchantment with politics and its potential of doing any good becomes more pronounced. "There is always a political interpretation to everything, but one shouldn't overdo it. . . . Since the normalization [in Greece] set in, we are looking for new approaches, and I have the feeling we are coming back to a kind of existentialism." And, just to show how Brecht is fading away, he adds: "The world is a chessboard on which man is just another pawn and his chance of an impact on the proceedings, negligible."

In Angelopoulos's second period he retreats into personal histories, though always keeping the greater canvas of history in the offing. He notes that during this period "history and politics move into the background . . . and the films focus more on the characters." Discussing *The Beekeeper* (1986) with Michel Ciment, he says: "We are now living a major historical moment, waiting for the world to change but having no idea how and when this is going to happen." Explaining the transition from the general to the personal, he uses a phrase that he repeats often in later interviews: "History is now silent. And we are all trying to find answers by digging into ourselves, for it is terribly difficult to live in silence." No wonder he sees in *Voyage to Cythera*, *The Beekeeper*, and *Landscape in the Mist* a trilogy of silence—silence of history, silence of love, silence of God (see Gabrielle Schultz's interview for *Die Zeit*).

To find the perfect visualization of this sentiment, one has to go deep into his third period, to a masterful sequence in *Ulysses' Gaze* describing the ultimate downfall of the communist dream in the grand funeral of a huge Lenin statue, tied down on a barge floating down the Danube. Peasants watching it from the shore uncover their heads and cross themselves—a clear indication that for them, communism and religion were not that different, whatever the official position of the party on that issue. Recently interviewed at home for this book, Angelopoulos said, "For many years, there was a strong belief the world could and should be changed for the better, and violent means were often used on both sides in the attempt to put down those who tried to bring about these changes." The annihilation of this dream is one of the sources for his bitterness. History was a disappointment. Those who believed in them, like himself, dearly paid for the ideals that could never come true. "My generation was severely hurt by this violent conflict. We lived in Greece a civil war that left behind a country in ruins, both material and spiritual."

The state of things today in Greece and in all the neighboring Balkan countries is the setting for the films of Angelopoulos's third period, which he describes as more existential, more centered on human fate. This period deals with borders, external and internal; exile, external and internal; the quest for a lost center—themes which recur like pieces of a great and painful elegy. In his last three films (*The Suspended Step of the Stork, Ulysses' Gaze, Eternity and a Day*), he sees the fate of his protagonists and, through them, of Greece itself as inseparable from the rest of the region in which they live. "Emigration and diaspora, refugees chased away from their own homeland, crossing borders and seeking shelter, these are among the most burning social issues of our time," he says. He may be referring to the catastrophes that have lately befallen this part of the world but which, he feels, are true on a universal basis. The title of the film *The Suspended Step of the Stork* refers to an officer who lifts one foot over the border and announces that if he puts it down on the other side, he will be shot dead. Borders are the evil to be abolished. "That was the real meaning of a united Europe, for me. The United States of Europe was our only hope to escape chauvinism and the hostility it breeds. Now it seems Europe is close to becoming one economic entity, but a united political entity seems very far away. And without it, it is very doubtful that an economic union can survive." Politics, once a major driving force for his creative juices, is further losing its flavor. On the set of his last film, *Eternity and a Day,* Angelopoulos tells Gideon Bachmann: "If you were to talk to me about politics . . . I would have to tell you that I understand less all the time and in the end I understand nothing."

The films of Angelopoulos are marked distinctively by his use of the sequence shot and by his obsession with cultural, historical, and political thematic matter. While these characteristics distinguish his films from those of his contemporaries, he has not emerged out of the blue. Angelopoulos often cites as inspiration the cinema of Michelangelo Antonioni. And, going further back, he mentions Murnau, Mizoguchi, Welles, and Dreyer, who all favored the sequence shot as much as he does. But none of these filmmakers has been as consistent in visual and thematic choices, and none could claim, as Angelopoulos rightly does, that all his films are basically episodes in one single piece of work, each one engendering the next. For this reason, he says, not one of his films finishes with the classic closing, "The End." And as long as he will continue to make films, the last word of each will be the first for the next.

Angelopoulos's film language is based exclusively on the sequence shot, and he is a strong believer in the "breathing shot," which should start a few seconds before the action it is supposed to depict and go on for a few more seconds after it is over. As he told Michel Demopoulos and Frida Liappas as early as 1974, while discussing *Travelling Players:* "The basic principle governing all the film is the sequence shot, whether the camera is moving (which it is most of the time) or immobile. This way, the scenes gain much in depth and detail, with the editing being done inside the camera." He insists that the sequence shots allow him much more freedom of expression, though, he concedes, it doesn't make life very easy for the audience. Originally, he says, the sequence shot was an instinctive choice, the only way he felt he could make films. Recently, after being asked once again to elaborate, he explained that for him, cutting real time into small time pieces, reaching immediately for the climax of each scene and eliminating the breath at the beginning and the end of each shot, is a bit like raping the audience, forcing one's vision on it. His camera embarks on long, intricate, and elegant movements that go on and on, observing the characters and the landscape in which they live from all possible angles, but always from a respectable distance, and rarely indulging in anything even remotely similar to a close-up. "I always fear those frames that practically scream 'Look at me!' "

Another visual aspect of his films is the pervasive barren landscapes of northern Greece, dark skies, rain, cold weather. He has been known to stop shooting when the weather improves, postponing the entire shoot for the next winter if he does not manage to wrap it up before spring. *Positif*'s Michel Ciment, one of his most ardent followers, suggested, when talking to him in 1987 about *The Beekeeper*, that this tendency reminds him of Antonioni's fascination with the valley of the Po River in northern Italy. Angelopoulos himself provides many possible reasons for this choice of landscape (some you will find in the interviews selected for this book) but finally concedes: "I have no explanation. I have often tried in the past to find one, but couldn't really. Maybe one has to look far back. A psychoanalyst might unveil the real sources."

Angelopoulos always shoots on real locations, never in a studio. In Greece there is not much of a tradition for studio work, and with his obsessive perfectionism, he does not even attempt it. But the actual locations, for him, are just a point of departure. "I feel the need to transform a natural landscape into an internal landscape that I see in my imagination. I have houses repainted, sometimes even relocated; I build bridges that haven't been there before."

The cutting in Angelopoulos's films baffles most traditional editors. Editing, as he has often pointed out, is done inside the camera, where the pace is established. The purpose of the editing table is just to check whether everything went on as planned on the set. If not, the scissors won't help. The only solution is to shoot the whole thing all over again. The only real editing in Angelopoulos's films is not for the image but for the sound, on which he lavishes enormous time and attention. "The sound effects are never accidental; they follow a certain cadence in relation to each other. One could almost count the beats. Do you know, for instance, that the actors were indeed counting silently between one line and another?"

Usually one of the roles of the editing process is to put a degree of order in the film's narrative so that it is more accessible to the audience. But for Angelopoulos the things he will not say are as important as the ones he does. "The ellipse is a tremendous option for the spectator to become the filmmaker's partner in the creative process." And for him, having the spectator as a partner is a condition sine qua non. "It all depends on the spectator and to what extent he is willing to do his share of the work when he watches my film. The film supplies him with a certain amount of information, but it is only by completing it with his own input that he can hope to enjoy the film." As far as he is concerned, no concessions are acceptable. Discussing with the editors of *Les Cahiers du Cinéma* the basic ingredients of *Landscape in the Mist*—two children on the road searching for their father—he almost fearfully remarks that "differently shot and putting these qualities in evidence, it could have been a tremendous commercial hit," an idea which evidently does not appeal to him at all.

Although the visual style is his most arresting feature, his thematic choices, his "obsessions," as he has been known to call them himself, are as easily identifiable: the search for a father figure, the importance of his presence or his absence, the father as a metaphorical concept and as a point of reference; the overwhelming importance of recent Greek and Balkan history and the way it affects the people who live in that part of the world, the attempt to recreate personal and historical truth out of fragments, little stories reflecting major historical events; the journeys all his characters embark on, the borders, the notion of exile, displaced persons searching for a place they can truly call home, and the trauma of the eternal return.

The accents of these themes may change as time goes by, as the following interviews clearly show, but they are present throughout his work. "All my obsessions enter and exit my films as the instruments of an orchestra do in a musical performance, they enter and exit, they fall silent only to re-emerge later. We are condemned to function with our obsessions. We make only one film. We write only one book. It's all variations and fugues on the same theme," he says in an interview made for the American press book of *Eternity and a Day*.

A recurring element in almost every one of his films is the frequent reference to Greek mythology, notably the *Odyssey*, which has supplied the basic dramatic structure for many of his films. "Greek people have grown up caressing dead stones. I've tried to bring mythology down from the heights and directly to the people" he tells Tony Mitchell, discussing *Megalexandros* (which refers to the Oedipal myth). Angelopoulos draws often from the *Odyssey* and from the myth of the Atrides, which was responsible for so much of the classic Greek tragedy. For instance, he has often mentioned that he sees the opening sequence of *The Reconstruction* as a modern replay of Ulysses coming home from his journeys. *Voyage to Cythera* is basically the story of Ulysses and Penelope, and of course, *Ulysses' Gaze* gives the mythological reference away in the title. The myth of the Atrides was used in *The Travelling Players* because it "offered the option of a social unit that I could observe all through the period from 1939 and 1952." The analogy is there, but never forced. The only name from the actual myth that he uses in the film is the name of the son, Orestes. As for the rest of the characters, he concedes that their motivations are different and the circumstances are not the same. "History affects them, changes and transforms them . . . this [the myth] helps me to define more accurately the historical space in which they are allowed to move."

It is interesting to note that up until his fifth film (*Voyage to Cythera* 1983), most interviewers focused on the purely intellectual aspects of his films.

They discussed in detail aesthetic decisions, political opinions, historical background, but rarely entered into the personal life of the director. It was a kind of reticence which might be interpreted as an expression of respect for someone who was revolutionizing the basics of his art—something very few, if any, of his contemporaries could claim to do. From *Voyage to Cythera* on, as the films themselves became more personal, so were the questions. He often pointed out that the opening sequence of this film, showing the German army marching into Athens, is based on an episode from his own childhood. Referring to the name of the father in the film, he tells Michel Grodent: "Spyros was the name of my father. For me, it represents his entire generation. In the context of the film it does not have any significance, but I am very much attached to it." No significance, indeed? "It is through the search for the father figure that we seek our way into the future and preserve our emotional balance," he says a bit later, in the course of the same interview. And as time goes by, it becomes evident that his personal history is intimately intertwined with the films he makes. As already mentioned, one of his most traumatic childhood memories is the deportation of his father after the war. His return is the inspiration for the first scene of his first film, *Reconstruction*. His leading characters often bear similarities to himself, as he will freely admit, and he sometimes reflects that "maybe I am simply limited to my own experience, my traumas and my hopes, my own personal growth and evolution."

Carrying the flag of the Greek cinema in the course of the last thirty years hasn't always been as pleasant an experience as one might imagine, particularly for someone as outspoken as Angelopoulos is inclined to be. He has openly criticized various aspects of the Greek cinema (and not only cinema). Many of his countrymen felt crushed under his personality and claimed he was obstructing their careers, leaving them no room to grow and develop on their own. Though at various times, the names of Cacoyannis, Kondouros, Voulgaris, and a few others gained a certain degree of notoriety, it is true that for the last thirty years, Angelopoulos has been practically the only one to consistently represent Greek cinema on the international scene. Naturally his long tenure at the top, over several generations, "has generated some bitterness, not only among filmmakers but also among film critics," as he is quick to point out. But he wasn't always as philosophical about it as he is today. He once remarked rather bitterly to Tony Mitchell that the catchphrase of the 1979 Thessaloniki Film Festival was "Death to Angelopoulos."

And this "love-hate relationship," as he calls it in the same interview, is not restricted to cinema only, for his criticism is directed at much larger Greek issues with similar results. Sometimes, he is exasperated enough to declare, as he did after *The Suspended Step of the Stork:* "I'd like to act just like Mastroianni in the film and announce that I am a political refugee in my homeland." And indeed, two films later, in *Eternity and a Day,* his hero, a poet who bears an uncanny resemblance to Angelopoulos himself, says he has lived all his life in exile. But, on the other hand, Angelopoulos accepts that "one can be critical of his own family without feeling the need to abandon it."

From the interviews in this book, one easily sees that in the early stages of his career he considered himself a full member of the Greek film industry. But both he and his interviewers stop relating to him as such the better known he becomes internationally. At home, some of the bitterness toward him was generated by the feeling that he is crowding all the national prizes and state subsidies. Unfair, claimed some of his colleagues, less famous and often having to struggle to find the budget for their next films. However, the budgets for his films—though barely shoestring productions by Hollywood standards—have been, for many years, too expensive for the modest Greek industry, and since *Megalexandros,* they have all been co-produced by his own company with Western European partners. True, the Greek Film Center is always a major investor, but they could hardly find a better investment. His films, as difficult as they are, still attract specialized audiences abroad, and in Greece, audiences still make quite a fuss about each and every one of them.

Most of the interviews for this volume were not originally published in English. Angelopoulos's insistence on film as art and resistance to the concept of film as entertainment has resulted in a very limited distribution of his films in Hollywood-controlled environments. In Europe, however, he is not only well known and appreciated; he is considered one of the pillars of modern cinema. This may explain why most of the interviews published here originated in countries that are familiar with his work and admire it, such as France, Italy, Germany or Israel, where most of his films since *Megalexandros* have had a commercial release. Everything you will read in the following pages has been translated at least once, more often twice. Since Angelopoulos himself speaks very little English, all his interviews are done either in Greek or in French, which he speaks perfectly. I realize the danger lurking behind the old Italian saying *traduttore-traditore* (translator-traitor). However, having known Angelopoulos for many years and having interviewed him quite often, I can say that it seems to me every single one of the interviews included here does represent his thoughts.

Two pieces of advice before you proceed to the interviews themselves. First, if you are just discovering Angelopoulos, you should probably start with the two Geoff Andrew contributions. Andrew is the senior film editor of the *London TimeOut* as well as a programmer of the National Film Theatre. Second piece of advise: these interviews shouldn't be read on their own. See the films, as many of them as possible, and you'll get so much more from the entire experience.

Many people have helped this project come true. First and foremost, I thank Theo Angelopoulos and his spouse, Phoebe Economopoulou (also his producer), who opened their archives and allowed me to choose the most interesting material I could find there. Angelopoulos graciously took the time to grant me a very long interview and kept me updated on every subsequent one he made after that. I am no less indebted to the Greek Film Center and Voula Georgakakou, who were always willing to provide information and material; to Elly Petrides, who put together the Center's booklet accompanying the British retrospective of Angelopoulos's films; to Karin Messlinger of the Berlin Forum, who gave me a hand with the translation of the Florian Hopf and Ulrich Gregor interviews; and to Gabrielle Schulz, who translated her own interview into English for my convenience. I would also like to thank my dear friend Alexis Grivas, who has been a source of information and has lent a helping hand on every occasion, without my having to ask for it. Without their assistance, I doubt if this work would have been ever completed.

And, of course, I would like to thank all of the original interviewers and publications that have graciously granted the permission to use their material in the present volume. And I am especially grateful to my wife, Edna, who has covered Theo Angelopoulos and his films as extensively as I have, contributing one of the interviews and all the advice I needed in order to complete this book.

CHRONOLOGY

1935 Born in Athens on April 27, to a family of merchants.

1940 First Italian and then German forces enter Greece. Some of these events find their echoes later in his films.

1944 Greece is liberated and enters a long and painful civil war whose wounds will take many years to heal. Father is arrested without warning, deported for no evident reason, and returns home nine months later, as suddenly as he has disappeared.

1959 Quits law school on the eve of graduation for compulsory military service.

1961 Having completed his army stint, he leaves for Paris to study literature, filmology, and anthropology at the Sorbonne.

1962 Enters IDHEC (Institut des Hautes Etudes Cinématographiques) and has conflicts there with his teachers; attempts to shoot a medium length film entitled *En Blanc et Noir* (*In Black and White*), which was never completed for lack of funds; negative is left at the laboratory.

1963 Moves from IDHEC to Jean Rouch's film courses at Le Musée de l'Homme.

1964 Returns to Athens; writes film criticism for *Democratic Change*.

1965 Works on a U.S.-Greek production of a fiction film on a pop group, entitled *Forminx Story,* which was supposed to serve also as promotion for the group's American tour. Replaced by the producers before completing the film.

1967 Military takeover of regime in Greece. *Democratic Change* is closed down; strict censorship enforced on all media.

1968 After two years and a long interruption in 1967 due to the political events in Greece, he completes *The Broadcast,* a b/w short about a radio show looking for "the ideal man." The film is screened and wins the Greek Critics' Award at the Thessaloniki Film Festival.

1970 *Reconstruction,* his first feature film based on an actual event, the murder of a Greek worker who comes back home from Germany, reaps most of the awards at the Thessaloniki Film Festival that year (best film, best director, best script, best actress, also critics' prize).

1971 *Reconstruction* is recognized abroad with the Georges Sadoul Prize in France and a special mention of the International Film Critics (FIPRESCI) at the Berlin Film Festival.

1972 *The Days of '36,* based on a real incident which took place in pre–World War II Greece, is best film in Thessaloniki; shown one year later abroad, the film wins the FIPRESCI award in Berlin.

1974 Starts his most ambitious project to date, *The Travelling Players,* in January. Because of political events he has to stop in May; he picks up again in November and the film is finished in January 1975. *The Travelling Players* collects even more awards than his previous films, not only in Thessaloniki, but also in Cannes, Berlin, Japan, and Brussels.

1977 *The Hunters,* the first film to be produced by his own company with French and German co-producers, is invited to the official competition in Cannes. Later that year, it is awarded a Golden Hugo in Chicago.

1980 *Megalexandros,* combining several Greek myths and fashioned in the form of a Byzantine liturgy, is a full-fledged co-production with other European countries, namely Italy and Germany; it wins Golden Lion and Critics Awards in Venice and later in Thessaloniki.

1981 *One Village, One Villager,* a documentary on a theme that has troubled him for many years, the fate of Greek villages abandoned by their inhabitants, is screened by Greek television.

1982   Invited to contribute to a series of documentaries on cultural capitals of Europe, he makes *Athens, Return to the Acropolis*, a personal vision of the city in which he was born and of its historical significance.

1983   Starts shooting in January *Voyage to Cythera;* stops for two months because of lead actor's poor health. Finished in 1984, the film starts a new cycle far more personal in nature, referring in a much clearer fashion to his own personal history. Shown a year later in Cannes, the film marks the beginning of a still ongoing partnership with Italian poet and scriptwriter Tonino Guerra and composer Eleni Karaindrou.

1986   *The Beekeeper* is shown at the Venice Film Festival. It is the first time he works with Marcello Mastroianni, who was to become a personal friend.

1988   *Landscape in the Mist* is unveiled in Venice, where it is awarded a Silver Lion. It is also selected Best European Film of the Year by the European Film Academy and one year later collects a Golden Hugo for best director and a Golden Plaque for best cinematography in Chicago.

1991   *The Suspended Step of the Stork*, with Mastroianni and Jeanne Moreau in the leads, opens in Cannes; starts yet another cycle in his work which he calls existential. His concern for the general state and the fate of the Balkan countries and his disenchantment with politics as such are brought very much into the forefront.

1995   Named Doctor Honoris Causa by the Free University in Brussels, Belgium.

1995   In *Ulysses' Gaze,* he directs for the first time an American star, Harvey Keitel. He shoots the film all over the Balkans, incorporating the past and present tragedies raging in this part of the world and the indelible link between them. The Cannes jury awards him its Grand Prix.

1998   *Eternity and a Day* wins the Golden Palm in Cannes and confirms his position, not only as an art film icon, but also as a major figure in the world of cinema. Following a long and often painful relationship with the Thessaloniki Film Festival, Greece's leading cinema event, which first acclaimed him, then damned him for crowding everybody else out of the picture, he comes full circle. He becomes the festival's president and as such, probably the most influential film person in the country.

1999   Awarded Doctor Honoris Causa at the Paris X University in Nanterre.

2000   Prepares new film, tentatively titled *The Third Wing*, a chronicle embracing the entire twentieth century and taking place on three continents.

FILMOGRAPHY

1965
FORMINX STORY
Director: **Angelopoulos**
Unfinished

1968
THE BROADCAST (I EKPOMBI)
Producer/director/screenplay: **Angelopoulos**
Cinematography: Giorgos Arvanitis
Editing: Giorgos Triantafillou
Sound: Thanassis Arvanitis
Cast: Thedoros Katsadramis (Ideal Man), Lina Triantafillou (journalist), Nikos Mastorakis (journalist), Mirka Kaladzopoulou (glamorous star)
B&W
23 minutes
Thessaloniki Film Festival—Critics' Prize

1970
RECONSTRUCTION (ANAPARASTASI)
Director: **Angelopoulos**
Producer: Giorgos Samiotis
Screenplay: **Angelopoulos** with Stratis Karras and Thanassis Valtinos
Cinematography: Giorgos Arvanitis
Sets: Mikes Karapiperis

Sound: Thanassis Arvanitis
Editing: Takis Davlopoulos
Cast: Toula Stathopoulou (Eleni Ghousis), Yannis Totsikas (Christos Grikakas), Michalis Fotopoulos (Costas Ghousis), Thanos Grammenos (Eleni's brother), Alexandros Alexiou (police inspector), **Angelopoulos**, Christos Palighianopoulos, Telis Samantas, Panos Papadopoulos (journalists), Petros Hoidas (judge), Yannis Balaskas (police officer), Mersoula Kapsali (sister-in-law), Nikos Alevras (assistant prosecutor)
B&W
110 minutes
Thessaloniki Film Festival (1971)—Best Director, Best Film, Best Cinematography, Best Actress, Critics' Prize
Hyeres Film Festival (1971)—Best Foreign Film
Berlin Film Festival (1971)—Special Mention FIPRESCI (International Federation of Film Critics)
Georges Sadoul Award (1971)

1972
DAYS OF '36 (MERES TOU '36)
Director: **Angelopoulos**
Producer: Giorgos Papalios
Screenplay: **Angelopoulos**, Petros Markaris, Thanassis Valtinos, Stratis Karras
Cinematography: Giorgos Arvanitis
Production design: Mikes Karapiperis
Music: Giorgos Papastefanou
Sound: Thanassis Arvanitis
Editing: Vassilis Syropoulos
Cast: Giorgos Kiritsis (lawyer), Christoforos Chimaras (government minister), Takis Doukakos (chief of police), Kostas Pavlou (Sofianos), Petros Zarkadis (Lukas Petros), Christophoros Nezer (prison warden), Vassilis Tsaglos (guard), Yannis Kandilas (Kriezis), Thanos Grammenos (Sofianos' brother)
Color
110 minutes
Berlin Film Festival (1973)—FIPRESCI Award
Thessaloniki Film Festival (1973)—Best Director, Best Cinematography

1974/75
THE TRAVELLING PLAYERS (O THIASSOS)
Director/writer: **Angelopoulos**
Producer: Giorgos Papalios
Cinematography: Giorgos Arvanitis
Production design: Mikes Karapiperis
Make-up: Giorgos Patsas
Sound: Thanassis Arvanitis
Music: Loukianos Kilaidonis
Choice of texts and songs: Fotos Lambrinos
Songs performed by Nena Mendi, Dimitris Kaberidis, Ioanna Kiourtsoglou, Costas Messaris
Editing: Takis Davlopoulos, Giorgos Triantafillou
Cast: Eva Kotamanidou (Electra), Aliki Georgouli (mother), Stratos Pachis (father), Maria Vassiliou (Chrysothemis), Vangelis Kazan (Aegisthus), Petros Zarkadis (Orestes), Kyriakos Katrivanos (Pylades), Yannis Firios (accordionist), Nina Papazaphiropoulou (old woman), Alekos Boubis (old man), Kostas Stiliaris (militia leader), Grigoris Evangelatos (poet)
Color
230 minutes
Cannes Film Festival (1975)—Grand Prix FIPRESCI
Berlin "Forum" (1975)—Interfilm Award
Brussels (1976)—Golden Age Award
British Film Institute (1976)—Best Film of the Year
Thessaloniki Film Festival—Best Film
Japan—Grand Prix of the Arts
Italian Film Critics—Best Film of the '70s

1977
THE HUNTERS (I KYNIGHI)
Theo Angelopoulos Productions with the participation of INA
Producers: **Angelopoulos**, Nikos Angelopoulos
Director: **Angelopoulos**
Screenplay: **Angelopoulos** with the participation of Stratis Karras
Cinematography: Giorgos Arvanitis
Music: Lukianos Kilaidonis

Editing: Giorgos Triantafillou
Sound: Thanassis Arvanitis
Production design: Mikes Karapiperis
Cast: Vangelis Kazan (Savvas), Betty Valassi (his wife), Giorgos Danis (Yannis Diamantis), Mary Chronopoulou (his wife), Ilias Stamatiou (Antonis Papadopoulos), Aliki Georgouli (his wife), Nikos Kouros (colonel), Eva Kotamanidou (his wife), Stratos Pachis (Giorgos Fantakis), Christophoros Nezer (politician), Dimitris Kamberidis (communist)
Color
165 minutes
Chicago Film Festival (1978)—Golden Hugo Award
Turkish Film Critics—Best Film of the Year

1980
MEGALEXANDROS
RAI, ZDF, Theo Angelopoulos Productions, Greek Film Center
Producer: Nikos Angelopoulos
Executive producers: Phoebe Economopoulos, Lorenzo Ostuni (RAI)
Director: **Angelopoulos**
Screenplay: **Angelopoulos**, Petros Markaris
Cinematography: Giorgos Arvanitis
Production Design: Mikes Karapiperis
Costumes: Giorgos Ziakas
Music: Christodoulos Halaris
Editing: Giorgos Triantafillou
Cast: Omero Antonutti (Megalexandros), Eva Kotamanidou (his daughter), Grigoris Evangelatos (teacher), Michalis Yannatos (guide), Laura de Marchi, Francesco Ranelutti, Brizio Montinaro, Norman Mozzato, Claudio Betan (Italian anarchists), Toula Stathopoulou, Fotis Papalambrou, Thanos Grammenos (community committee), Christophoros Nezer (Tzepelis), Ilias Zafiropoulos (young Alexander)
Color
210 minutes
Venice Film Festival (1980)—Golden Lion for Best Film, New Cinema Award, FIPRESCI Award

1981
ONE VILLAGE, ONE VILLAGER (ENA CHORIO, ENAS KATIKOS) (documentary)
Greek Armed Forces Television (YENED)
Director: **Angelopoulos**
Cinematography: Giorgos Arvanitis
Editing: Giorgos Triantafillou
Sound: Thanassis Arvanitis
Color
20 minutes

1982
ATHENS, RETURN TO THE ACROPOLIS (ATHENA, EPISTROFI STIN ACROPOLI) (documentary)
Trans World Films, ERT TV, Theo Angelopoulos Productions
Director/writer: **Angelopoulos**
Texts: Costas Tahtsis
Cinematography: Giorgos Arvanitis
Music: Manos Hadjidakis, Dionyssis Savopoulos, Lukianos Kilaidonis
Poetry: George Seferis, Tassos Livaditis
Editing: Giorgos Triantafillou
Sound: Thanassis Georgiadis
Production design: Mikes Karapiperis
Color
43 minutes

1983
VOYAGE TO CYTHERA (TAXIDI STA KYTHIRA)
Greek Film Center, ZDF, Channel 4, RAI, Greek Television, Theo Angelopoulos Productions
Producer: Giorgos Samiotis
Executive producers: Samiotis, P. Xenakis, Phoebe Economopoulos, V. Licuressi
Director: **Angelopoulos**
Screenplay: **Angelopoulos** with Thanassis Valtinos, Tonino Guerra
Cinematography: Giorgos Arvanitis

Production design: Mikes Karapiperis
Costumes: Giorgos Ziakas
Music: Eleni Karaindrou
Sound: Thanassis Arvanitis, Dinos Kittou, Nikos Achladis
Cast: Manos Katrakis (old man Spyros), Giulio Brogi (Alexandros), Mary Chronopoulou (Voula), Dionyssis Papayannopoulos (Antonis), Dora Volanaki (Katerina, old Spyros's wife), Athinodoros Proussalis (police captain), Michalis Yannatos (coast guard officer), Vassilis Tsaglos (president of the dock workers' union), Despina Geroulanou (Alexandros's wife), Tassos Saridis (German soldier)
Color
137 minutes
Cannes Film Festival (1984)—Best Screenplay Award, FIPRESCI Award

1986
THE BEEKEEPER (O MELISSOKOMOS)
Greek Film Center, Greek Television (ERT-1), Marin Karmitz Productions (France), Basicinematografica (Rome), Theo Angelopoulos Productions
Executive producer: Nikos Angelopoulos
Director: **Angelopoulos**
Screenplay: **Angelopoulos** with the participation of Dimitris Nollas, Tonino Guerra
Cinematography: Giorgos Arvanitis
Music: Eleni Karaindrou
Editing: Takis Yannopoulos
Sound: Nikos Achladis
Production design: Mikes Karapiperis
Cast: Marcello Mastroianni (Spyros), Nadia Mourouzi (the girl), Serge Reggiani (the sick man), Jenny Roussea (Spyros's wife), Dinos Iliopoulos (Spyros's friend)
Color
120 minutes

1988
LANDSCAPE IN THE MIST (TOPIO STIN OMICHLI)
Greek Film Center, Greek Television (ERT-1), Basicinematografica (Rome), Theo Angelopoulos Productions

Director: **Angelopoulos**
Screenplay: **Angelopoulos** with the participation of Tonino Guerra and Thanassis Valtinos
Cinematography: Giorgos Arvanitis
Editing: Yannis Tsitsopoulos
Music: Eleni Karaindrou
Cast: Tania Palaiologou (Voula), Michalis Zeke (Alexandros), Stratos Tzortzoglou (Orestes)
Color
126 minutes
Venice Film Festival (1988)—Silver Lion for Best Director, FIPRESCI Award, Art Cinema Association (CICAE) Prize, Pasinetti Award
Chicago Film Festival (1988)—Golden Hugo Award, Best Cinematography Award
Felix Award for Best European Film of the Year (1989)

1991
THE SUSPENDED STEP OF THE STORK (TO METEORO VIMA TOU PELARGOU)
Greek Film Center, Theo Angelopoulos Productions, Arena Films (France), Vega Films (Switzerland), Erre Productions (Italy)
Producers: **Angelopoulos**, Bruno Pesery
Executive producers: Phoebe Economopoulos, E. Konitsiotis
Director: **Angelopoulos**
Screenplay: **Angelopoulos**, Tonino Guerra, Petros Markaris, in collaboration with Thanassis Valtinos
Cinematography: Giorgos Arvanitis, Andreas Sinanos
Production design: Mikes Karapiperis
Costumes: Giorgos Patsas
Edited: Yannis Tsitsopoulos
Music: Eleni Karaindrou
Sound: Marinos Athanassopoulos
Cast: Marcello Mastroianni (politician who disappeared), Jeanne Moreau (his wife), Gregory Karr (Alexander, the journalist), Ilias Logothetis (the colonel), Dora Chrysikou (young bride), Vassilis Vouyouklakis (production director), Dimitris Poulikakos (television cameraman)
Color
126 minutes

1995
ULYSSES' GAZE (TO VLEMA TOU ODYSSEA)
Theo Angelopoulos Productions, Greek Film Center, MEGA Channel, Paradis Film, La Générale d'Images, La Sept Cinéma with Canal+, Basicinematografica, Instituto Luce, RAI, Tele-Muenchen, Concorde Films, Herbert Kloider and in association with Channel 4
Producers: Giorgio Silvagni, Eric Heumann, Dragan Ivanovic-Hevi, Ivan Milovanovic
Executive producers: Phoebe Economopoulos, Marc Soustras (Paris)
Director: **Angelopoulos**
Screenplay: **Angelopoulos** with the participation of Tonino Guerra, Petros Markaris, Giorgio Silvagni
Cinematography: Giorgos Arvanitis
Music: Eleni Karaindrou (violin solo: Kim Kashkashian)
Editing: Yannis Tsitsopoulos
Sound: Thanassis Arvanitis, Marton Jankov-Tomica, Yannis Haralambidis
Production design: Giorgos Patsas, Miodrag Mile Nicolic
Cast: Harvey Keitel (A), Maïa Morgenstern (woman in Florina, Penelope, Kali/Calypso, widow/Circe, Nausica), Erland Josephson (Ivo Levy), Thanassis Vengos (taxi driver), Giorgos Michalakopoulos (Nikos), Dora Volanaki (old lady in Albania), Mania Papadimitriou (mother in A's memory)
Color
176 minutes
Cannes Film Festival (1995)—Grand Prix, FIPRESCI Award
Felix for Best European Film of the Year (1995)

1998
ETERNITY AND A DAY (MIA EONIOTITA KE MIA MERA)
Theo Angelopoulos Productions, Greek Film Center, Greek Television (ERT-1), Paradis Films SRL, Intermedia SA, La Sept Cinéma with Canal+, Classic SRL, Istituto Luce, WDR, ARTE
Executive Producer: Phoebe Economopoulos
Director: **Angelopoulos**
Screenplay: **Angelopoulos** in collaboration with Tonino Guerra, Petros Markaris
Cinematography: Giorgos Arvanitis, Andreas Sinanos
Editing: Yannis Tsitsopoulos

Music: Eleni Karaindrou
Sound: Nikos Papadimitriou
Production design: Giorgos Ziakas, Costas Dimitriadis
Costumes: Giorgos Patsas
Cast: Bruno Ganz (Alexander), Fabrizio Bentivoglio (the Poet), Isabelle Renauld (Anna), Achileas Skevis (the boy), Alexandra Ladikou (Anna's mother), Eleni Gerassimidou (Urania), Iris Hatziantoniou (Alexander's daughter), Nikos Kouros (Anna's uncle), Alekos Oudinotis (Anna's father), Nikos Kolovos (the doctor)
Color
132 minutes
Cannes Film Festival (1998)—Golden Palm Award for Best Film, Ecumenical Prize

THEO ANGELOPOULOS
INTERVIEWS

An Elegy for a Land Rotting Away: *Reconstruction*

FLORIAN HOPF/1971

Q: *Let's start with your premises and intentions.*
A: This case, for it is a real case, intrigued me. I had noticed several stories of this kind in the Greek papers dealing with women who had murdered their husbands. And in Epirus, the poorest and most backward region of our country, this seemed to be particularly frequent. I decided to go to the village in which a recent murder took place and investigate the case from the point of view of a journalist. I spoke with the inhabitants, with the family of the accomplice, with the children, and with the defendant's lawyer, who opened before us the minutes of the trial. This was the basis for my script, which used the murder as an excuse to portray life in a small Epirian village. Since I was not personally involved in the crime, not even as a witness—I was just a visitor from a big city in search of information—I felt it would be dishonest of me to turn it all into a fictional account. Something like Visconti's *Ossessione*, which deals with a similar story. *Reconstruction* tries to approach the case on two different levels. The first offers as accurate a version as possible of the events, based on the testimonies I had collected myself and on the minutes of the trial; the second level is the police reconstruction with the participation of the guilty parties. The film functions, therefore, as a confrontation between the official version put together by the authorities and my version, presented in the form of a questioning. The plot moves constantly between these two elements in a manner that is quite different from a logical

---

From the catalogue of the *Internationales Forum des Junges Films, Berlin* 1971. © 1971 by Internationales Forum des Junges Films. Reprinted by permission. Translated by Dan Fainaru.

narrative. To give you an example, the film concludes with a scene that should have been at the very beginning: the murder itself. But what exactly happens there is still a mystery, because the camera remains outside, never witnessing the deed itself, just hearing the voices.

Q: *It seems you were not particularly concerned with the legal aspects of the case.*
A: Certainly not. The real issue for me was to watch this doomed region whose fate threatened to become that of the entire country.

Q: *Does this mean you attempt to explore the historical background of this region, its social structures . . .*
A: Certainly not. To begin with, there is no social or economic structure to speak of in that area. The simple truth is that the only money available there is the money sent home by the people who had emigrated to Germany. This film, for me, is an elegy for a land rotting away, abandoned by its inhabitants. It all started in 1962 when West German subsidies included the permission for Greek citizens to live and work in Germany. This issue was hotly debated at the time by both the right-wing and left-wing papers in Greece. Some claimed emigration is nothing less than a disaster; others believed it was rather positive, for if many workers went away, there would be no danger of an organized working class and therefore no resistance to the regime in power. The Colonels prefer, these days, to see all their opponents leave the country. All my friends, for instance, live abroad . . . unless they are in prison. It is for them that I made *Reconstruction*. For all those who have already left and those who are about to. And there is something else. Epirus has a rich and very old history and culture, its roots going back to antiquity. It is terribly sad and upsetting to watch impotently as so many people are leaving this land, for once they go away, a whole civilization ceases to exist.

Q: *How did they survive there before the wave of emigration.*
A: Of course it wasn't easy, but one way or another, they did it. In any case, Greeks are a nation of emigrants. At the turn of the century, half of them went to America. There are one and a half million Greeks in the U.S. There are already 300,000 in Germany. They are everywhere, and instead of contributing to Greek economy at home, they are working for others. The Americans are coming into Greece now, claiming they wish to industrialize the country, but of course they will do it only if it is profitable for them. And

Greece, for many, is now the fifty-first state of the Union. Five months ago, two Americans raped a sixteen-year-old Greek girl. They were acquitted when they came up with the perfect alibi: they were never in Greece, they hadn't left the States at all.

Q: *You are implying Greece is a Third World country.*
A: That is the way things are. The Third World is not limited to Africa and Latin America. If you ask me, it includes Greece and Turkey too. We do not belong to the West, we are not part of Eastern Europe—we live at the crossroads of modern civilization. However, we happen to occupy a strategic point in the Middle East; therefore, we are important to American politics. Had it not been the case, their attitude towards us would have been completely different.

Q: *How was Reconstruction produced?*
A: Like every other independent production in Greece. To begin with, the producer is not really a producer; he is a film technician. He works for commercial productions but is a socially conscious person. He worked, for a while, with the professional unions, but not any more. He wants to do something else. All we had, when we started *Reconstruction,* was a small investment, contributed by a cousin of his and another friend. Altogether, when we started shooting, the budget was on the order of something like 2,500 German marks, but before we finished, it went up to 46,000 marks.

Q: *Any previous experience as a director?*
A: I made a short that was highly praised by the critics, about the alienation created by radio, television (though we still don't have it in Greece), and publicity. But let's go back to *Reconstruction.* We started with a crew of five persons: the producer, the cameraman, an assistant cameraman, a production manager who also filled in as script editor, and myself. There were only two actors, neither one of them professionals. One of them was a barman, the other, unemployed. He had been sent to jail for political reasons and once released, after two years, couldn't find any work. We were the first to offer him a paying job. All the other people in the film are peasants we found on the spot. Even the woman who plays the lead is an amateur; in real life she is a seamstress. I chose her because she fit the part, not physically, but psychologically. She was great, but she couldn't either read or write.

Q : *Did you write down the dialogue and have the actors learn them by heart or did you rely on improvisation?*
A : Everything was written beforehand, most of it before we started shooting, and then inserted into the script. There isn't one improvised line in the film.

Q : *How did you manage on such a small budget?*
A : Well, it was like this. We had 9,000 meters of raw material, and we had a soundman who claimed he could manage without an assistant. Once he set up his equipment, he would handle the microphone and trust the tape recorder to work without supervision. We shot for twenty-five days, regardless of the weather. As a matter of fact, it was raining most of the time, so we didn't have much of a choice. We were invited to stay with the peasants in their homes, and we somehow managed to scramble some food. Lights, there were none. Only a handheld lamp, a 500 kw transformer, two batteries, and a small, portable power generator rented for the occasion. We also had a small truck we used to move our equipment around and sometimes to sleep in.

Q : *What are the conditions of Greek cinema today?*
A : My film has the lowest budget of any film produced in Greece. But it is not one of a kind. There was a time when cooperatives were making films on very low budgets. In most cases, for this kind of film, the persons involved have to use their own money. There is no State subsidy and no producer who would be interested in a film like mine. And it's a pretty risky business, too. Whoever puts his own money in a film and doesn't get it back—as it is mostly the case—will never do another film. Three or four major companies control the Greek cinema and distribution, and they are not interested in this type of film.

Q : *How many films are annually produced by these companies?*
A : It varies—from fifteen to a maximum of thirty for each of these companies. These are pretty expensive productions, all of them featuring the Greek stars of the moment.

Q : *How many cinemas do you have in Greece?*
A : Plenty, because we still do not have television. There are some 200 cinemas in Athens only, and close to 2,000 all over the country.

Q: *How was* Reconstruction *received in Greece?*
A: The press screenings were tremendously successful and everybody was convinced that it would be a box-office success. But the trouble was that I couldn't find a cinema to show it in. The exhibitors had made up their minds to boycott it.

Q: *Who are these exhibitors?*
A: All sorts of people, united in their common interests with the distributors. They make a lot of money by keeping their screens available for the people who provide them with films all year long.

Q: *Do you mean you have theater chains controlled by major producers, who are showing only the films made by these producers?*
A: To find a distributor, someone like me would have to hand the film over to him. But since distributors realize that such a film would compete with their own productions, they prefer to forget it on the shelf.

Q: *How many films are made in Greece, altogether?*
A: Overall, we have an annual production of approximately 120 films. But many of them are never released in Athens; they go into general release without a proper first run. You have to keep in mind that Greece still has many analphabetics, people who cannot read subtitles. Also, in Greece the entire family goes to the movies, which means that any film restricted to adult audiences is automatically doomed to fail. Therefore, the only option is to make family pictures, where adults can go with their children.

Q: *What did finally happen to Reconstruction?*
A: Some 650,000 people have seen it until now. To put it in perspective, films featuring our leading stars reach 1.5 million admissions.

Q: *Anyway, your performance is quite remarkable. Do you believe it could have done even better?*
A: Let's consider a simple fact. I am showing my film in one cinema, not very central, while the others are releasing their films on fifteen screens. Even if it is a flop, there will still be a few hundred people, living next to the cinema, who will come to see it. Doesn't seem to be very much, but it counts, nevertheless.

Q: *Do you mean that no distributor will accept the fact that a film he hasn't produced could generate profits?*
A: I have screened *Reconstruction* for the biggest distributor in Greece. After ten minutes, he stood up and said, "I am not interested." He didn't even stay till the end. But it is quite possible I will find a big distributor for my next film, on one condition: that he believes there is a chance of selling it abroad.

Q: *How about censorship?*
A: We were not sure that once the film was finished, it would be cleared by the censors. As a matter of fact, we feared they would ban it. Therefore, I first screened the film for the critics.

Q: *Before the censors had seen it?*
A: Exactly. The next day, they all wrote that they had seen a masterpiece. Because of this enthusiasm, the censors had to let it go. They did not feel like running the risk of a public outcry in case they banned the film.

Q: *Did they touch it at all?*
A: No, but we had quite an argument with the Ministry of Interior, who wanted to cut it.

Unveiling the Patterns of Power:
The Days of '36

ULRICH GREGOR/1973

Q: *What is the historical background of your film?*
A: It is based, more or less, on real facts. A convict used a gun to take hostage a right-wing Member of Parliament who visited him in his cell. Later it turned out the two knew each other for a long time, though the nature of their relations was less than clear. Was there some kind of agreement between him and the convict? Nobody knows. The convict writes to his friends: "I am going to kill him and then kill myself; there are no documents proving they have ever arrested me." But since the hostage was a pretty well known personality, the case triggered a very complicated reaction. There was great anguish in the political circles, particularly in the right, since the hostage was one of them. The government was directly concerned. I should mention that at the time, General Metaxas was ruling the country. He had acceded to power through the support of the right wing and center that had joined forces in his favor. Neither one of the two could rule the country on its own, since they had an equal number of votes, while Metaxas himself had only seven seats in the Parliament and the communists had fifteen. Since the two leading parties wanted to keep the communists out of the game, they agreed to let Metaxas take over. This Metaxas was a great admirer of Mussolini and had all sorts of shady dealings with Goebbels, who made a special trip to Greece just to visit him.

From the catalogue of the *Internationals Forum des Junges Films, Berlin*, 1973. © 1973 by the Internationales Forum des Junges Films. Reprinted by permission. Translated by Dan Fainaru.

Q: *Did the murder of the union leader have anything to do with the case?*
A: No. I introduced it into the story. That is, I put together a number of events. The jail incident is a true one, and so is the murder of the union leader, though it happened a bit later. I put them together to give a better idea of the political climate during that period. The plot, however, is concentrated in the space of a few days only.

Q: *A few but very significant days, they represent the entire period.*
A: Exactly. It is perfectly clear I am dealing with a time in Greek history when the actions of the workers parties were beginning to become effective. Strikes and demonstrations were everyday occurrences. Briefly, the kind of climate that would be difficult to describe today, given our political situation. Going back to Metaxas, the two parties had enthroned him despite his being a real fascist, following in the tracks of earlier previous dictators. He did not make any effort to dissimulate his positions, and he had no scruples declaring that under his guidance, Greece would never face the risk of another autocracy. The King (joining forces with Metaxas and the British) wanted stability at any price, even if this meant opening the door to a dictator.

Q: *And indeed, you have an Englishman in your film.*
A: Yes, and he talks about dictators and interventionism. "As far as I am concerned, I am against any strong-arm intervention," he claims. Theoretically, maybe. For he adds: "I have to agree however that there are certain situations . . . in a number of underdeveloped countries . . . ," and he never finishes the sentence. But it is clear from his tone that he is in favor of intervention.

Q: *Do you think the Greek audience identifies the characters in your film? For instance, do they recognize Metaxas?*
A: No doubt about Metaxas. Also the Member of Parliament. The character in my film is very close to the real person. He is vaguely homosexual and that is how I portrayed him. He is very elegant, has a certain kind of body language . . . briefly, he is easy to identify. No wonder the real person, who is still very much alive, is furious.

Q: *Given these elements, the audience may very well draw some up to date conclusions?*

A: It is true that our present political situation is not unlike the time when the King intervened in favor of Metaxas, after realizing the two leading parties were unable to reach an agreement on their own. The kind of political situation that could lead to a takeover by a certain Mr. X, just like it was the case with Metaxas.

Q: *How did you manage to produce the film?*
A: One of my friends used to teach at the Greek Film School. He had a student whose husband—a rich man—was an admirer of *Reconstruction*. He said he would like to finance one of my films, and I took him up on the offer, that's it. We became friends and shared the same political opinions. His political awareness vastly changed as we were making the film. He told me later: "I don't care if I lose money on your film. The experience was worth it, through this film I learned a lot of things I did not know before." He wasn't the type of producer who would say, "Your film didn't make a penny." I used the same crew I had in *Reconstruction,* slightly larger since there was a bit more money. Some of the actors were professionals, the rest amateurs.

Q: *Do the Greek censors read the script or do they only look at the finished product?*
A: Scripts are supposed to be checked by the censors, but we managed to slip it through. To tell you the truth, there is quite a bit of difference between the original script and the film in its final form. The scene of the Englishman was not in script, nor the murder of the union leader. As a matter of fact, there was no mention of a union leader, just of some person who had been murdered.

Q: *Once finished, did the film encounter any censorship problems?*
A: Some. I prefer not to go into details; it would be silly of me, since I have the intention of continuing to make films in Greece. The main thing is that *The Days of '36* was released.

Q: *I believe the first screening was at the Thessaloniki Film Festival.*
A: Indeed, and it was enthusiastically received by the audience and the left-wing parties. The ones who were really angry were the center parties. They felt my portrayal of the parliament at the time was embarrassingly suggestive of the present regime of the Colonels.

Q: *Who are these people?*
A: Neither the liberals nor the center left. These are the people who lost all their privileges after the Colonels rose to power, and this includes some of the right-wing people. The parliamentary regime generated a certain number of social changes. People with vast fortunes have seen their profits curtailed and lost their place to others. Government officials are being paid the double of what they made before. The same for the police, whose condition before had seemed hopeless. Since many were forced to retire, there were plenty of possibilities to grab a government office.

Q: *Are we talking about a class of bureaucrats?*
A: Exactly.

Q: *I understand the screening of Reconstruction by the German television has been of great help to you.*
A: True. And the same goes for the prize I was awarded in France. Also the screening of the film by BBC in England. Greece is a small country; for them I am now an important person. Someone with an international reputation you can't throw arbitrarily into jail.

Q: *Does it mean there is a chance for artistic and cultural activity in Greece today?*
A: In any case, we're trying to work in this sense. . . . Take for instance *Synchronos Kinematographos,* a film magazine in which I am not personally involved. It could be easily defined as a para-marxist publication, at least it is evident to me.

Q: *Your film's style is very elliptical. There is always something the audience won't find on the screen and will have to fill in on its own.*
A: It's one way to go beyond naturalism, as Dreyer used to say. The ellipse is a tremendous option for the spectator to become the filmmaker's partner in the creative process. It also offers a kind of "Brechtian alienation" that depends not only on the position of the camera, but also on the structure of the film. Every film is made up of a number of individual blocks that—to use Brecht's definition—are autonomous, but they all depend on each other. The point, evidently, is to follow an almost naturalistic course in order to better underline the realism of each sequence. For instance, by striking a certain

pose, the character about to be murdered breaks through the apparent naturalism of the moment and becomes realistic.

Q: *This apparent naturalism is evident in the very careful way you draw each one of your characters.*
A: With an intentional pinch of irony. I tried to use satire for the portrait of this bunch of goons that were ruling the country. Also, I had to keep in mind the formula of political cinema that emerged after the films of Rosi and Costa Gavras. *The Days of '36* is the opposite of *Z*. In Gavras's film there is a clear distinction between heroes and villains. The same goes for the situations. Everything is predictable, it fits in with the middle-class ideology. My films are trying to be more hybrid, without a beginning or an end. I attempt to introduce a sort of "anti-suspense" ritual, something of the kind Oshima created in *Death by Hanging*, recently released in Greece.

Q: *You mentioned earlier Dreyer, even quoted him. Have his films had any influence on your work?*
A: No. The only film of his I know is *The Passion of Jeanne d'Arc*. *Dies Irae* is being released now in Greece but I haven't seen it yet. I read some of his declarations in the Greek press, and I was referring to them. If you are looking for an affinity, it is more in the direction of Godard you should look. He had a certain influence on me . . . and on the other filmmakers of my generation. At the early stages, there was also a touch of Antonioni, and then Godard.

Q: *I heard there is a new generation of cinephiles in Greece, and they are interested in modern cinema.*
A: True. We get to see now all the important new films, like Oshima's *The Ceremony* or Straub's *Othon*. It doesn't matter whether they like them or not, the main thing is that they discuss them. In a few days, we'll have a strike here, caused by the competition between cinema and television. The theaters are empty, and the strike will protest against the exorbitant taxation of the cinemas. These type of demonstrations are familiar in Western Europe, but in Greece they are just beginning.

Q: *I'd like to go back to your film. What is the significance of the boys distributing leaflets?*

A: It's another reference to the political climate at the time. Since it was prohibited to distribute leaflets, they had to be given away like this. In the context of the film, it is supposed to mean that on the one hand there is a law, but on the other hand, there are young people willing to take the risk and challenge it. It's another way of underlining certain aspects of the regime.

Q: *Three government officials are shot in the last scene.*
A: Executions were by hanging, before the dictatorship. But in practice, they killed people any old way. Public opinion found this out only after the demise of Metaxas, during WW2.

Q: *What about Pindar's text?*
A: Mussolini ransacked Roman classics for his fascist propaganda; in Greece fascists did the same with Greek classics. During Metaxas's stay in power, they used to refer to the three great civilizations. The antiquity, the Byzantine era, and the Metaxas civilization. They quoted old texts that no one understood to justify their positions—it was all a mumble-jumble of meaningless words, nothing more.

Q: *The film is often ambiguous. For instance, who is the murderer of the union leader?*
A: No one knows. All we know is that the suspect was one of the persons who shot at the people marching. The point was not to show who pulled the trigger but to indicate that he has done it together with many others who could be considered equally responsible.

Q: *Your film does not offer a concrete analysis of the political facts, in the current sense of the word. There is a lot you left out, to be completed by the audience, and this adds to its ambiguity.*
A: Indeed, for, as I said before, what I was looking for was a certain climate. A reign of terror. People claim their innocence by accusing an innocent person. No one achieves his purpose. The patterns of power are unveiled as they reach their inexorable conclusion—to kill. For me, this is shocking: the state eliminates a person without giving him the benefit of a court of law to prove his innocence. All means are acceptable—poison, for instance—as long as it terrifies the people.

Q: *There is a certain similarity here with the American gangster movies. Some of the characters seem to be lifted out of them.*
A: True. The murderer is dressed just like the gangsters in the thirties. The reference is even clearer, because the person is a policeman but at the same time, he is one of the gangsters, known in the underworld as "Valentino" because of his resemblance to the movie star. In the picture, whoever tries to speak up is immediately wiped out. Only the diplomats are free to express themselves. The same goes for the mother of the MP, but then she is one of the rich and powerful. No one would touch her.

Q: *Class struggle?*
A: I prefer to avoid this cliché. The film deals with a certain, specific class at a certain, specific point in history. The previous generations were freedom fighters, while their sons. . . ." There are many families of this kind in Greece. After WW2, they married into money, bringing for their dowry the reputation of their name. Let's face it, the fate of Greece is decided by no more than 200 families. Onassis, for example, intended to put up a temple in the center of Athens in memory of his son, as if the city of Athens belonged to him. . . .

Q: *Was The Days of '36 finally released commercially?*
A: Yes. Some 50,000 admissions in Athens and altogether I believe we'll reach 100,000 in the entire country. For Greece, it isn't very much.

Q: *Did you get any state subsidies?*
A: Not a penny. But they did not forget to collect the taxes, which in Greece are 50% of the ticket price.

A Journey through Greek Landscape and History: *The Travelling Players*

MICHEL DEMOPOULOS AND FRIDA LIAPPAS/1974

Q: *When did you decide to shoot* The Travelling Players, *and what were the political circumstances at the time?*
A: We launched the film during the so-called liberalization period of Markensinis, that is on the eve of the Polytechnic events. In any case, since the film deals with the 1939–52 period and refers to all sorts of unmentionable historical episodes, the Papadopoulos censors wouldn't have been very likely to approve it. Nevertheless, we decided to go ahead and shoot the film. Shortly before we started, the Polytechnic incidents erupted in all their violence followed by the Ioannides putsch. At this point we wondered whether it was worth making a film that might very well never be shown in Greece. And what would be the sense of such a decision? We discussed the matter with the producer, and he agreed with us that even if the film was to be banned in Greece, it would achieve its purpose through the echoes of its screenings abroad. In January and February 1974, as the terror was reaching its peak, we decided to go ahead with the film. We were prepared to make our film disregarding any censorship threats whatsoever.

Q: *What was the original idea?*
A: I first thought about a travelling company touring the smaller towns around the country. A journey through the Greek landscape and history, following a group of actors from one town square to the next. Later, more

---

From *Synchronos Kinematographos*, no. 1, Sept. 1974. © 1974 by Synchronos Kinematographos. Reprinted by permission. Translated by Dan Fainaru.

elements were added like, for example, using the myth of the Atrides for the relations between the actors. I used an existing formula—father, son, mother, lover, their children . . . power . . . murder—which functions both as a myth and as a basis for the plot. It was a liberating decision, since I had made up my mind from the very beginning this was not supposed to be a lesson in history. The myth of the Atrides offered the option of a social unit that I could observe all through the period from 1939 to 1952. *The Days of '36* revealed the portrait of a dictatorship. *The Travelling Players* is a kind of sequel, giving names and specifications to this portrait. It goes up only until 1952, because I believe that year's massacres put an end to the civil war and consecrated the triumph of the right wing and the victory of Papagos. That is, the story covers the period between the overt dictatorship of a general to the veiled dictatorship of a field marshal, who was viewed by many Greeks, exhausted by all the catastrophes they had experienced before, as a liberator. There were a number of obstacles I had to overcome in order to achieve my purpose. First, to combine all these elements into one structure, but also to avoid conventional scenes of the kind you encounter so often in these circumstances: hunger, death, persecutions, etc. For this reason, the film begins in 1952 with Pagagos's election campaign. I wanted to portray the generation of the Resistance, the people who were against the Metaxas dictatorship, who fought in WW2, who joined the National Front of Liberation and retreated later into the mountains. All those who were forced by the events to take a stand and, finally, were considered the "Resistance generation" from the leftist point of view, naturally. Three persons represent this generation in the film: the older 1939 militant and two younger persons suspected of sympathizing with this man and his opinions. All three of them join the Resistance and are arrested. One of them is deported and released in 1950 after signing an anti-communist declaration. The second is executed in 1951 for refusing to give up the armed struggle. The third falls ill in prison, is released for "health reasons," and will carry with him the "revolution trauma" for the rest of his life. Time has stopped for him in 1944; he constantly projects the events of that year into the future. The entire picture bears the stamp of this trauma. All the characters suffer from it. Some have signed the declaration, others have died in prison or lost their minds.

Q: *You claim you used the myth of the Atrides to avoid the artificiality of a conventional arbitrary form. Aren't you worried that such a myth, so deeply entrenched* in the cultural traditions of our civilization, would create an opposite effect, by imposing on the film an inexorable fatality? You obviously wish to use the myth as an historical model, but it could lead to the wrong conclusions. Some people might take the film as another interpretation of the myth.

A: To begin with, the presence of the myth is not that evident in the film. We do not use names, there is no Agammemnon, no Electra, no Pylade, not even a Nikos or Pavlos. The only name in it is Orestes, who for me is a concept more than a character: the concept of the revolution so many dream of. The affection many of the characters lavish on him represents their yearning for the ideal notion of the revolution. Orestes is the only one who remains faithful to himself and his goals, and is willing to die for them.

Q: *Isn't there a risk in identifying your protagonists with the heroes of the myth (Electra, Orestes, Egistus, Agammemnon, Clitemnestra) and then placing them in a different historical context?*

A: The motivations are different, the circumstances are not the same. History affects them, changes and transforms them. All I did is sketch them, and this helps me to define more accurately the historical space in which they are allowed to move. In the film, Egistus is a militant for the August 4 party and finds himself involved in pseudo-collaboration with the Germans. The concept of power is revealed in him by his attitude to the other actors, after the death of Agammemnon. Attempting to analyze his personal motivation would lead to a psychological drama about the primal reasons that made Egistus what he is. And that does not interest me at all. What I was trying to achieve is a kind of Brechtian epic, where no psychological interpretation is necessary.

Q: *How did you put the script together? How did you use the myth in it?*

A: First of all, I tried to use the 1952 events as a point of departure. From that point, I looked back, but not in the classical flashback tradition, because these are not personal recollections of one definite character, but collective memories, giving me the freedom to plant inside the 1952 sequence certain historical episodes from the past. The first scene takes place in 1952, the last in 1939. As you can see, I am progressing in the opposite direction. In the final scene we see all the characters who participate in the film. Some of them, we know, have been already killed in action; others are in jail. The survivors are old by now; they have broken up, have been barely released from prison. They walk towards each other, they stop in front of the camera, and we hear the text of the beginning: "In the summer of 1939 we reached Aigion. We were exhausted, we hadn't slept for two nights." The only difference is the year—instead of 1952 in the opening scene it is now 1939. The characters here are still full of hope for the future, but we know what is in store for them. It's like an old family picture we look at, knowing only too well what is going to happen to each of the persons in it.

Q: *How did you select the historical events you wanted to show on screen?*
A: The choice of some dates and events is evident at first glance. The first "historical fact" we run into, in 1939, is the declaration of WW2. This "fact" affects everybody and is therefore introduced at a popular festivity, the actors and many other people being there at the same time. The German victory is represented by the capitulation of a small Greek garrison. The Liberation is seen through a popular revolt. Later, in December 1944, we have the measures against possession of weapons, the civil war, and the elections of 1952. Also, when selecting the events, I preferred those I found to be most representative of Greek characteristics. For the 1944 events, it was the people in the street and the dimensions of their reaction I was concerned with, not the governmental decisions as such. The people consider December 1944 as their revolution, a revolution that was cut off in the middle, before it reached its natural conclusion. Why? My film does not offer a straightforward answer to the question, but there is plenty of evidence in it to find the answer. For instance, why didn't the ELAS [The Greek Popular Army of Liberation] reach Athens? And there are more events we all know are part of the historical background of that period. Everything is shown through the perspective of simple people—the same people who have to bear the effects of these events. The film is a popular epic much more than an analysis of recent Greek history.

Q: *Unlike your first two films, the erotic element is of major importance in* The Travelling Players. *What is its significance in relation to the political elements in the picture?*
A: The sexual element is integrated in the characters. Clitemnestra's affair with Egistus and Electra's reaction are all based on their respective personalities. There is however a point when these relations stop being only personal, for Egistus is more than just the lover of the mother. He is also a traitor. He

is killed not only because of his affair with Clitemnestra or because he has successfully ridded himself of Agammemnon, but for betraying Agammemnon and his son to the Germans. Electra's rape is a political act as well. I believe that at the origins of every act of violence there is some kind of sexual impulse. Since Electra is raped in interrogation, the act becomes automatically political. The film also introduces the concept of prostitution. Chrysotemis is a prostitute who later marries an American soldier. This kind of marriage may solve a certain problem, but at the same time it represents the bankruptcy of moral values. The sexual element is therefore transferred to a political-ideological level.

Q: *What does the stage play* Golfo the Shepherdess, *produced by the players in your film all over Greece, mean to you?*
A: The play functions on several levels. First, it is the means for these players to make a living. But it is also art, since they perform it on stage. Then there is the text they use and the myth of the Atrides. The text is always interrupted at some stage and never completed on screen. And finally, adding the historical background, the play itself gains another dimension. Let's take, for example, one line from the play: "Are we being watched?" This doesn't have anything to do with the popular drama anymore; it refers to the fate of the actors themselves, the characters of the film.

Q: *It seems as if* Golfo *is the only play they ever perform. And you have to agree that both thematically and dramatically this is a very conventional play. Politically speaking, it rather mystifies instead of clarifying the true antagonism between social classes. Don't you feel there is a contradiction between the distinct political position of the actors themselves and the reactionary ideology of the play they keep producing?*
A: *Golfo* in nothing more than a convention, a Greek version of *Romeo and Juliet*. The actors are not really conscious of the conflict between their personal politics and the ideology of the play. All they want is to make a living by offering their audience the kind of fare they like to see.

Q: *What about the relations between theater and cinema? The stage sequences raise the question of realism, in the sense that an actor plays an actor who plays a role in a play, so what is real in all this?*

A: I have given a lot of thought to this matter. The actors play actors. Masks, costumes, sets, they are all extremely important elements. The change of costumes, for example. When the Englishman puts an actor's beret on his head and gives the actor another hat in exchange, he becomes an actor in the play as well. When the British perform on the improvised set or sing "Tipperary," the actors are the audience. When Golfo is supposed to fall down, dead, a British soldier falls too, killed by a bullet, as if he, at this specific moment, was playing the part of Golfo. Certain acts and events are repeated all through the film and given more than one sense, and the performance of the play is never concluded because it is always interrupted by the political events taking place at the same time.

Q: *Does your film adhere to a clear esthetic concept established beforehand?*
A: Despite rumors that I have a definite esthetic concept with which I will stick through hell and high water, I would like to insist on the fact that I do improvise a lot. In the film there are a certain number of very dynamic scenes featuring a large variety of actions, and also static scenes, the three monologues. Since I wanted to have one distinct esthetic approach, I tried to compensate through camera movements in every possible instance, except for the theater production and the three tales. For these scenes, the camera stood still, facing the actors. The basic principle governing all the film is the sequence shot, whether the camera is moving (which it is most of the time) or immobile. This way, the scenes gain much in depth and detail, with the editing being done inside the camera. We never shot two scenes, if we had the option of doing it in one.

Q: *You feel much more comfortable with the sequence shot and prefer it to the traditional editing process.*
A: It is my own notion, possibly a very personal one. The sequence shot offers, as far as I am concerned, much more freedom, but it is true that the spectator needs to be more involved in it. There is another advantage I like in the sequence shot that you cannot have in traditional editing: the empty screen, when the action is implied, taking place elsewhere.

Q: *We could say the sequence shot adopts the concept of montage but instead of using traditional editing, it combines together various elements in one scene, which, through the movement of the camera, stimulate the imagination of your spectators.*

A: It is equally important to mention that through the sequence shot it is possible to preserve both unity of space and unity of time. The film does not acquire an artificial pace at the editing table. Also, once you change the frame, it is as if you're telling your audience to look elsewhere. By refusing to cut in the middle, I invite the spectator to better analyze the image I show him, and to focus, time and again, on the elements that he feels are the most significant in it.

Q: *Did you encounter any difficulties during the production of the film?*
A: First of all, the weather. I was persecuted by beautiful weather. I needed a clouded sky—I couldn't imagine the occupation under sunny skies. But Greece is well known for its magnificent weather and sunny sky, summer and winter alike. You can't imagine how much trouble this was! When you have scenes where the first part is shot in Athens and the second in Amfissa, you need to have similar meteorological conditions; the mood, the atmosphere have to be as close as possible. And that is rarely evident in a film. On top of that, we went over budget, and worst of all, we were afraid of shooting this kind of film under the present conditions you are only too familiar with.

Rhythms of Silence to Better Underline the Scream: *The Hunters*

FRANCESCO CASETTI / 1977

Q: *How did you prepare for this film?*
A: To begin with, we had a script that was barely more than a sketch, a kind of extended synopsis. Then I started searching for the right locations—I always choose them myself, even if this means travelling extensively all through Greece. In *The Travelling Players* it was somehow easier because the story itself kept moving from one location to another. In *The Hunters* everything takes place in one spot, a hotel, which makes the choice much more difficult. Once I found it, I went ahead and wrote the shooting script, always leaving a margin for improvisation. Though there isn't much room for improvisation here. Once I started working on the set, we rehearsed every single scene for three full days and only then went ahead and shot it. We had some sequence shots of seven to eleven minutes each; consequently there was no room for errors or improvisations. The slightest mistake meant we had to start the shot all over again. And that takes a lot of time. The rehearsals were pretty systematic: first the actors, then the camera, then the sound. . . .

Q: *The camera set-ups were finalized beforehand or did you make up your mind as you were working on the scene?*
A: For the camera movements, I usually followed the indications of the shooting script. But whenever I felt it was necessary, because of a conflict between them and the position of the actors, I did not hesitate to make the

From *Cinema e Cinema*, no. 13, Oct.–Dec. 1977. © 1977 by Francesco Casetti. Reprinted by permission. Translated by Dan Fainaru.

necessary changes. To make it clearer: in early rehearsals, the actors were pretty free to choose the way they moved and then I corrected the things I was not comfortable with and condensed the action. My intention, from the very beginning, was to avoid at any cost a realist effect, to reach some kind of pure geography. That is, to stress the evidence of the film direction, its artificial side—the opposite of an opinion I heard, claiming the film is realistic. Like the American musicals with their breaks between musical numbers and the plot, creating on purpose an artificial cinema by the way they were directed. Working with the actors, in this respect, was of major importance. Having to keep their distance from their roles, in the Brechtian tradition, doesn't make their job any easier. On the contrary. We had to insist on their penetrating under the skin of their characters, without showing it. We were trying to achieve a kind of minimalist effect in the spirit of the Japanese theatre which uses the rhythms of silence to better underline the scream.

Q: *Does it mean the performances had to be purged of any trace of pathos?*
A: Yes, just like I did in certain passages of *The Travelling Players*. The three monologues delivered directly into the camera, were "dried out" of emotions in order to achieve a kind of alienation that would have been ruined by realistic performances. In *The Hunters* I went one step further: this film is cold—at no point can the audience identify with the characters or does it wish to. The actors are not supposed to reflect a distinct personality; they should be like masks. Just like classic theatre that, next to the immobile masks, used the voice to express the emotions. I would like to add that I was also trying to achieve a kind of musicality—to give the script the form of a musical score. The sound effects are never accidental; they follow a certain cadence in relation to each other. One could almost count the beats. Do you know, for instance, that the actors were indeed counting silently between one line and another? The point of departure was realistic but from there on I let the rhythm dictate the procedure. The film acquired a musical structure.

Q: *That means the film is not really as "cold" as you suggested, it has its "hot" aspects.*
A: It all depends on the spectator and to what extent he is willing to do his share of the work when he watches the film. The film supplies him with a certain amount of information, but it is only by completing it with his own input that he can hope to enjoy the film. The pleasure derived will not be

the result of its "beauty" only, but also of the feeling that what it shows is really "intolerable." In this sense, the film is "cold" on the first level, but very hot on the second. This is a terribly sad film, an unpleasant film that rejects all relief stemming from easy hopes. It is a film about the present we live in, about how things seem to stay the same as if nothing had happened despite all the political changes taking place around us. My earlier films worked on several levels, too, but here I believe it is much clearer. The scene in which the girl makes love with the imaginary king, the father-king, the God-king, is drawn out to such length that it becomes unbearable and fascinating at one and the same time. What I am trying to say is that fascination enters the picture here only on a second level, once the viewer has done his share. This film is not supposed to deliver all its secrets on first sight, it is only through your own dialogue with the screen that the picture is completed.

Q: *In this sense,* The Travelling Players *could be defined a "hot" film on the first, immediate level. Also, it had a compact style throughout. In* The Hunters, *it seems as if every single moment has its own "tone."*
A: For instance?

Q: *For instance, you never before used a device like the clapboard preceding the scene of the actress-singer. Or the love scene that leads into a completely different direction.*
A: True, I used them to break into the rhythm and also into the thematics of the film. The second scene you mention is a long sequence shot showing two people making love, a group sitting around the table eating, the American woman walking in and offering to buy everything, the politician undressing. By moving from one to the other in one sweeping camera movement, we reveal the many facets of one central situation and at the same time prevent the viewer from identifying with any of these facets, since he is jolted from one surprise to another. This way, we multiply one aspect while canceling another. This is what Brecht meant by alienation. I would also like to point out the way I matched shots—systematically using every possible variant from the classic visual matching through sound matches and interior/exterior matching of shots. The point was to deny these matches their natural function and to bring into the open all the artificial aspects of film direction. This is clearly a show put on for the benefit of the

audience, there is no realistic excuse to explain it, like the theatre in *The Travelling Players*...."

Q : *Which unified the various levels of the picture...."*
A : Here the matching is far more violent to prevent any type of identification. In this respect, *The Hunters* is a much more materialistic film than *The Travelling Players*. The direction is far more evident. I would also like to draw the attention to the aggressive structure of the film which should jerk the audience out of its complacency.

Q : *Another thing. The empty screen, as it was used in* The Travelling Players, *was, for me, a moment of reflection, waiting for the character to complete his action.*
A : In a certain sense, you are right. But if we use once more the musical score as a model, these dead moments are the equivalent of musical pauses. After the last note, there is a moment of silence, allowing the viewer to grasp the sense of the entire sequence. Normally, shots are cut when the action is over, or the last sound is heard. Emptiness, the dead moment, is the impression you have when there is nothing more to show or to hear.

Q : *It's like pauses used in certain types of modern jazz. Not just a moment of suspense, but a device whose purpose is to underline the rules of the game.*
A : True.

Q : *Recently, I had the occasion to see again* The Days of '36 *and found there a similar approach.*
A : Some of my films are "hot," others are "cold." The hot ones are *Reconstruction* and *The Travelling Players*. The cold ones are *The Days of '36* and *The Hunters*.

Q : *Two final questions about your narrative approach. First, I was amazed by the lack of chronological references in* The Hunters.
A : In *The Travelling Players*, the chronology of the film relies on important historical events, familiar to most people. Here, however, the various periods are introduced through aspects of internal Greek politics that non-Greeks will find difficult to identity. But in any case, it is true that I do not pay much attention to specific dates. I suppose it would have been possible to clarify

the plot chronologically speaking, but I didn't do it because this is neither an historical film nor a film about history. The dates are irrelevant. Nothing really happens in that hotel, except passing emotions, nightmares, twisted gestures of blind precision. The exact historic references are less important. My intention was to concentrate on the persons inside that hotel, who represent in my eyes the composite conscience of a certain generation and certain social class.

Q: *The second question. In* The Travelling Players, *the relations between the characters was familiar—parents, children, friends, lovers and so. Here however. . . .*
A: Here they are hardly mentioned. The characters are divided into couples, man/woman, man/woman. This doesn't make it any easier for the audience, for there are no clear ties between the characters to rely on. But I do not believe there is any need to specify the nature of these ties, for all the characters are various facets of one single person. I would like to stress again the film is the process of one single conscience, taken at various degrees.

Q: *Somehow, I felt as if all the characters were participating in a mysterious plot, whose nature is not divulged.*
A: Without the expansion of the time element and the "dead moments," this could be compared to Hitchcock's *The Trouble with Harry,* which shows various characters trying to get rid of a corpse. But expanding to the extreme the time element is the opposite of everything a typical moviegoer expects to see in the cinema. Still, if it were up to me, I would like to show *The Trouble with Harry* and *The Hunters* together.

Animating Dead Space and Dead Time: *Megalexandros*

TONY MITCHELL / 1980

You've described classical Greek antiquity as a millstone the Greek people are forced to bear. Is O Megalexandros *an attempt to draw on a more popular, political mythology?*

THEO ANGELOPOULOS: Greek people have grown up caressing dead stones. I've tried to bring mythology down from the heights and directly to the people, in both *The Travelling Players* and *O Megalexandros*. The title is not "Alexander the Great," but "Megalexandros," who exists in popular, anonymous legends and fables, and has nothing to do with the historical Alexander—he evokes a totally different personage. For this reason we have had difficulty finding a translation for the title. The legend of Megalexandros originated in 1453 under Turkish domination, and it has come down through oral tradition over the centuries. It embodies one of the deepest of Greek sentiments, that of waiting for a liberator, even a Messiah—he's a kind of Christ figure, and in the film is also identified with St. George.

The film is based on two sources. One is "The Book of Megalexandros," which is an account of the legend, and provides the general climate of the film rather than the storyline. The second, more concrete source is an actual event in 1870, when a group of aristocratic English tourists were kidnapped by Greek bandits at Marathon. The bandits held them ransom and demanded an amnesty from the government in exchange for the hostages. The government botched the whole business, and the exchange never came

From *Sight and Sound*, Winter 1980/81. © 1980 by Sight and Sound. Reprinted by permission.

about; so the tourists were killed and a scandal erupted. The British fleet blockaded the port.

This is your third film in which British characters appear, albeit in relatively minor roles. In Days of '36 *and* The Travelling Players *they appear as caricatures to English eyes. Do you see them as paternalistic colonial oppressors? One critic even used the word "xenophobic" about* O Megalexandros . . .
When I use English characters, they are not so much representatives of Britain as of all foreigners, from the point of view of the Greek people, or the common consciousness, which has regarded the British as a governing force operating from outside. After all, up to 1947 Greece was dominated by the British in the role of protectors. Stylistically, they are caricatures, and forceful ones, of the foreign colonizer, the exporter of capital from Greece. But if you caricature someone, it does also imply a certain affection, a sympathetic acceptance. The tourists in *O Megalexandros* are innocents, especially Lord Lancaster, who was related to Queen Victoria. He's an innocent, Byronic type, in love with Greece; but he is outside the responsibilities of power and has no real weight politically.

The long and drawn out process of editing the film would seem to suggest it is on a similarly epic scale to The Travelling Players. *Is it as complex in its dislocation of time and cross-references?*
The first thing to be said is that it's the most simple film I've made so far. Its progress is linear, and it hasn't developed its stylistic form in the course of editing like the other films. There are no chronological jumps—the film begins on New Year's Eve in 1900 and proceeds from there, except for the final sequence when the little Alexander becomes Megalexandros and goes towards the city. Which is a modern city—present-day Athens, in fact—in contrast to the rural, turn-of-the-century world of the rest of the film. When the little Alexander enters the city, he brings all the experience of the century with him. He has gained a total experience of life, sex and death, and he comes into the city at sunset, and over it there is a great question mark. How long will the night last, and when will a new day break?

Does this mean the film is more realistic than The Travelling Players?
On the contrary—it's more surrealistic. It doesn't describe real events, but

their sense and meaning, and concentrates on political and sexual consequences. It's a more "poetic" film, whereas *Travelling Players* was more concrete.

Eva Kotamanidou's role seems very complicated—she is Alexander's sister, daughter and mistress . . .
Her role is a result of the structure of the "Book of Megalexandros," which intertwines a number of myths, such as Oedipus, but under different names. In the popular legend, which the film follows, Alexander's birth is a mystery; he is a "child of fortune," so he adopts a woman from the town as his mother, and her daughter becomes his sister. Later he marries his adopted mother, so his stepsister becomes his stepdaughter. In the film, the story of this marriage is told by a narrator. On the wedding day, assassins hired by the landowners try to kill Alexander, but they get his wife/mother by mistake. Her bloodstained wedding gown remains beside the bed. It is all the daughter has to identify her mother with, and she wears it when Alexander has her executed.

Was your decision to cast Omero Antonutti as Alexander an attempt to give the film more of an international focus?
No. I'd seen him in *Padre Padrone* and was struck by his physical features, which seemed appropriate for the part. After all, the actor is only a vehicle in a film, which has to stand or fall on its own merits.

You have now taken over your own production. Is this due to distribution problems as well as the difficulty of finding a backer? The Hunters, *for example, has had very little European release, which was surprising after the success of* The Travelling Players.
I went into production because there was no Greek producer prepared to put up enough money for my films, which do need a big budget. I didn't want to produce *O Megalexandros,* but it was a case of necessity. I don't know why *The Hunters* had such a restricted release; a possible, hypothetical reason may be that some critics saw it as a Stalinist film, which certainly isn't true, and is a very subjective and superficial reading.

You said recently in an interview that you see yourself as an isolated presence in Greek cinema, with little contact with other directors.

I think that other Greek directors don't have the same problems as I do. Being Greek, I am part of Greek cinema, but not in the localized, provincial sense; and as far as style is concerned, there's no meeting point. The catchphrase of the 1979 Thessaloniki Film Festival was "Death to Angelopoulos." I'm in a privileged position, being well known, and this perhaps causes communication problems for others with me, but not vice versa! But I do have rather a love-hate, father-son, psychoanalytical relationship with Greek cinema. Also I'm not a member of any political party, because I find that the Left in Greece now speaks a dead language.

You have said that you find it more difficult to make a film in Greece now than it was under the Colonels.
That's not a question of the Colonels being more cruel and repressive, but of my rapport with power. My films are very much about the problems of power, and they are political only in so far as the problems of power are political. Under the Colonels there was a clear antithesis; there was more cohesion among the people who resisted, and more coherence on the Left, whereas now it is scattered and in disarray. To give an example—the Colonels gave me permission to film inside the old Parliament, whereas now I can't get that permission. *Days of '36* is more successful now than it was at the time I made it because it conveys the sense of the silence of censorship imposed by the Colonels.

Your consistent use of tracking shots since Days of '36 *has caused critics to talk about the influence of Jancsó, who now seems to have dispensed with the technique. Do you see any danger of its use becoming too arid or mechanical?*
I deny that I have been influenced by Jancsó! *Plan séquence* (sequence shot) has existed throughout the history of cinema—in Murnau's films, for example. The way that Jancsó uses tracking shots isn't real *plan séquence;* there is a fundamental difference between his use of it and mine, which I think is its real use. When I use *plan séquence,* it is to create a complete, finished scene, with inherent dialectical counterpoints. The scene is concluded, whereas in Jancsó's films there are *plans séquences* which are long, but they don't amount to finished scenes. His are lateral, and convey only one meaning. As for the technique being mechanical—you don't criticize a writer for having a particularly idiosyncratic, personal style.

Do you see plan séquence *as a way of arriving at a kind of alienation effect?*
Not in the sense that there is any manipulation involved. I've always been irritated by the way that montage is such an artificial process, dictated by a cinema of efficacy. For example, a man enters, stops, and waits. In the cinema of efficacy this waiting is conveyed through montage, whereas in my work there is no montage—the scene exists in a time scale which is not reduced for the sake of efficacy. There is a material, concrete sense of time; real time, not evoked time. In my films "dead time" is built in, scripted, intended. Just as music is a conjunction of sound and silence, "dead time" in my films is musical, rhythmic—but not the rhythm of American films, where time is always cinematic time. In my films the spectator is not drawn in by artificial means, he remains inside and outside at the same time, with the opportunity of passing judgment. The pauses, the "dead time," give him the chance not only to assess the film rationally, but also to create, or complete, the different meanings of a sequence. As far as the question of influences is concerned, I draw techniques from everything I've seen, but the only specific influences I acknowledge are Orson Welles, for his use of *plan séquence* and deep focus, and Mizoguchi, for his use of time and off-camera space.

Have you any plans for a new film?
Editing O Megalexandros has been such a difficult and laborious job that I haven't had time for any future plans. I've had an offer from RAI, the Italian television network, to make a film about Magna Grecia, and also a number of suggestions from Germany about theatrical and operatic projects, which I find particularly strange, as I've never worked in the theatre before.

The Growing of Tomatoes

GIDEON BACHMANN/1984

Q: *Do you find in your work that sometimes there is a battle between perfection of form and the content, the thing you want to say?*
A: I don't think so. I know that one could suppose that what is known as maniacal search for perfection requires a tremendous effort, but I feel that the choice of locations, of sets, of the time of shooting, and the director of photography are in themselves enough to make the work less difficult. In the end, once you are there, it's as simple as breathing. If there is a battle of the kind you mention, it happens very rarely.

Let's take an example. In *Voyage to Cythera* there are three successive shots of an old man dancing. It is in a cemetery. The three shots are on the same axis. The first is the beginning of the dance, the second is a continuation of the dance and, at the same time, the discovery of the space around, the third is the arrival of the son who says, "these women are waiting for you to open the house." At the same time, it also accentuates distance, since the third shot is from further away. I had a problem with these shots, but I finally accepted them. It was a series of shots against the light. Shots against the light usually create a kind of metaphysical beauty. This happens, for instance, in Bergman's *Seventh Seal* . . .

Q: *. . . or in* Earth *by Dovzhenko, where there is a dance shot against the moonlight.*

Unpublished interview. Cannes, May 1984, following the screening of *Voyage to Cythera* in competition. © by Gideon Bachmann. Reprinted by permission.

A: Exactly. The question was whether to accept this quality or reject it. Finally, I decided to accept it. Especially in the second shot where the purpose was to express a character that related in some way to the sky, the backlighting was useful.

Q: *Are you saying that visual elements are, in any case, only means of expressing content? A question of syntax? You speak your film language, the question is, does the spectator understand it?*
A: I don't think there is a solution for this problem. In the kind of cinema I make, which is always a linguistic research, you arrive at a point where language becomes content. It is possible that the spectator can only follow with difficulty. It is a matter of dosage. I am in favor of giving the spectator a first chance at an interpretation, and I construct a second or a third level which may be perceived by a more advanced spectator, but I believe in a first level that can be read with relative ease. At least, that is what I am trying to do, but there is always the question whether I succeed to achieve my purpose. I do not function like a computer and I cannot plan everything. There is a tendency to believe that directors who make more complicated films program them in great detail, but for me it is still a question of instinct. It is possible that the director who plans more has a greater impact on the spectator. You feed in all the factors—a bit of humor, a bit of drama—you concoct a proper electronic cocktail and feed it into a calculator which will then supply a recipe for an image, good or bad. But I don't think, for example, that Fellini works like that.

Q: *I suppose you could go all the way back to the question whether cinema, which costs a lot of money and needs to be seen by a great mass of people, is the best medium for those who do not like to work with this kind of cocktail. Those who have something to say, whose ideas go beyond the first level of reading. Obviously, you have chosen to answer this question affirmatively, you have decided to believe that cinema is a medium for ideas. In fact, there seems to be a growing public on your wavelength. But don't you feel worried sometimes that there will be too many who are not?*
A: I can't worry about that. Every single day, new kinds of different publics are born. Outside the big American films which attract automatically because of their ability to communicate through the medium with a large public, there are quite a few other groups of cinema goers, more of them everyday.

Q: *Are you working with a specific public in mind?*
A: There seems to be something . . . there are people who buy my films and look a them, not many perhaps, but it is a kind of public. However I do not believe you can do something well if you try to transform a medium of expression into a desperate cry for communication.

Q: *"A desperate cry for communication" is a very beautiful definition for art; why then have you chosen an art that is so expensive? Why not music, painting, writing, talking . . . ?*
A: I sometimes ask myself this question. Perhaps because I was told, when I went to cinema school that I was a genius . . . that I should continue. So I continued.

Q: *In other words, is it because you felt accepted in this area?*
A: No, but it is a taste one acquires. The cinema is a disease. It outlasts the times when one is not accepted, as well. I have had a very difficult time in the past. But the cinema is very strong—one cannot live without it. It's not just a medium of expression; it's a form of life.

Q: *Could we see, then, the character of Alexander in your new film, as an alter ego, on a certain level? In his office, he has a poster of* The Travelling Players *on the wall, and in the best sense, also I believe that all the important films are autobiographical. Yours, Tarkovsky's, and Fellini's, anyway. To my mind, you are the three directors who succeeded in personalizing this industry. But I find in the character of Alexander a somewhat diminished energy. There is a reticence, a feeling of disillusion with his own profession. Does all this relate to a certain extent to something actually happening to you? Is this your 8½?*
A: Yes, I suppose you read it correctly. Sometimes it becomes very hard to go on, very discouraging. There were a number of times, in the course of making this film, that I wanted to stop the production. People are constantly asking me why it took such a long time to make. There are two answers, both valid. The first is that the main actor got sick and we had to wait for him. The second is the weather; it was not at all favorable and yet we went ahead and created the feast as a symbol. And I felt more than once that continuing to make the film was a symbol too. Often I felt the urge to end the film with a question. That is the real reason for the delay. I was having problems with myself.

For me, filmmaking is not a profession. I do not feel I am a film professional. I could live otherwise. So why? In order to talk to someone, to communicate? In order to go to Cannes? To win prizes? To travel? To live a director's life? No. That's not it at all. My inner need during this production, when I felt like stopping it, was to go to the country and do nothing. So this whole film came into being during a period in my life when I was going through a personal crisis. What an easy thing to say—an excuse for anybody. But it relates to something in me.

Q: *The strength of the film lies, I think, in the fact that this can be felt.*
A: I lived through a period of severe political disappointment. I know we all went through this, but I was seriously marked by it. It was perhaps the strongest shock I have suffered. That, of course, played a role in this film.

Q: *So the little dance everybody asks the meaning of is just what I thought it was: an affirmation of life, a continuity rite?*
A: It's taken from a children's game. There are black squares and white squares and you're not supposed to step on the lines separating the squares.

Q: *Memories of childhood, the ease of one's relationship to reality which memory procures, are very useful in moments of crisis and that's how I saw it. The dance as an element of survival while everything around him—women, love, theater, etc.— had begun to leave him cold.*
A: One has the feeling—and I discovered it while I was shooting this film— that this man is saying goodbye. Leaving on a trip which is at the same time a trip for a film. *Voyage to Cythera* is probably the kind of film he was supposed to make. That is the first level. But, of course, the metaphor is clear . . . , it is as if he was really leaving for a trip and saying goodbye. To his home, to his mistress, to the people around him, to everything that is his. Like leaving a message on his answering machine, saying "I'm gone to Cythera."

Q: *But surely, you will continue making films?*
A: I have a great desire to make another film very fast. I think I have never wanted so badly to make another film, as I do now. This one was a sort of deliverance, of liberation.

Q: *I had no problems with this film, unlike my experience with* Megalexandros *and* The Hunters, *in both of which I felt there was an inner conflict and a somewhat tortured soul at work. I also find that in* Voyage to Cythera *you are sending the old man to die with little equivocation, accompanied by his Comsomol Nausica.*
A: It is Alexander who sees the departure of the two old people, and it is as if he was sending them away. That's the liberation. Cutting the umbilical cord.

Q: *Is it the communist ideology you are sending away to die?*
A: That's a very simple way of putting it, somewhat schematic. It's a whole historical period that had become an obsession, a trauma. The period which created the disillusion I had mentioned before. Lost illusions. For me, in the film, the man is finally lucid. He has his identity crisis, he is seeking himself, but there is clarity in him.

Q: *Why have you isolated him to such an extent, why haven't you given him the support of another person?*
A: Because he has to find the solutions for his problems on his own. That's his only choice. Nothing and nobody can help with that. Not love, nor anything else on the outside. It's the essence of his own being, the autonomy of existence.

Q: *But you speak of the desperate cry for communication. I am aware that the philosophy of the moment states that one can't offer anything if one isn't anything, or rather that one cannot give if he is not. My own tendency is to think that "to be" means to be in touch with another being. Or more than one, but one will do. God wouldn't have destroyed Sodom if there had been more than one single righteous man in it. So to be alone is not enough. How can there be communication and feeling? After all, we are a tribal animal.*
A: The problem of being must be solved by each person on his own. But in the creative process, "to be" means "to understand" before anything else. To understand yourself. In creation, in order for communication to take place, there have to be at least two beings. What happens between people is creation.

Q: *But in* Voyage to Cythera, *Alexander seems to have accepted the idea that he can't communicate with anyone.*

A: You will remember there is no final title in the film, saying "The End." I think this is a film to be pursued farther. It is the same with the films of Fellini and Antonioni; they are never finished. I have, and I think the spectator has, the feeling that there are more images to come, but one doesn't know yet what these images are going to be. I myself do not know what Alexander is going to do next.

It is true there is a feeling of renunciation in the film but also of a new departure. A departure that all one knows of is the trip itself. It's not really a *Voyage to Cythera*, it is more like *Embarking for Cythera*.

Q: *There is, then, a conflict between the fact that, as you say, some people see and buy your films and the fact that you do not know who they are. The film becomes a surrogate for hope.*
A: I hope to be able to contradict you. During the dictatorship, I traveled from town to town, all over Greece, invited by students, film clubs, in big cities and in the smallest villages, projecting and discussing my films. I did it for *Reconstruction, Days of '36,* and *The Travelling Players*. The last film I did it for was *The Hunters*. I don't need to do this kind of thing anymore these days. During the dictatorship it was very useful and very necessary. It was a form of real communication beyond what is normally possible in cinema. I did know my public then. The film was not a surrogate but a vehicle.

Q: *Does the urge you have to do another film quickly correspond to the sense of liberation Alexander has at the end of* Voyage to Cythera. *The feeling of being able finally to say what he really and effectively feels, and if so, what is it that you really and effectively feel now?*
A: To the first part of your question the answer is definitely yes. The answer to the second part of the question is still to be discovered, but to be discovered without the anguish that stalked me until now.

Q: *That was exactly my feeling. I thought that the little dance he does, which we discussed before, is the beginning of another film. Maybe of another life. I don't know you—before today I did not know you have a wife, how you lived, who you were—but the film gave me the feeling that what was to follow was a life of greater joy, of a closer contact with nature. I don't know, cats maybe . . .*
A: In fact, I started to grow tomatoes.

A Withered Apple: *Voyage to Cythera*

MICHEL GRODENT/1985

Q : *Let's start with the credits sequence. Is it supposed to have a mythic dimension?*
A : For me, this sequence leads to a dream world, underlined by the music that seems to reach us from the outer spheres. Its purpose is to indicate right away the dreamlike state the film was conceived in. The following sequence shows the little boy as if he has landed from another planet. Though, to tell you the truth, I can't really give you an exact interpretation of the credits—I did it this way because I liked it, without very precise ulterior motives. I can't point out any strict logical reason for it.

Q : *The episode of the boy and the German soldier looks like a childhood memory.*
A : Yes, it is, but it is very clearly a filmed memory, to wit the director's voice. [Angelopoulos's own, D. F.] at the end of the sequence, giving instructions to the boy. Farther on, the camera looks through the window and discovers the city landscape, as if through a kind of frame. A man wakes up, goes to the child whose name is now Alexander—in the dream sequence his name was Spyros, and we later find out this is also the name of his grandfather. I am trying to imply, of course, that my protagonist, who is a film director, used the image of the boy for the fictional presentation of his own childhood. The audience must realize, from the very first moment, through the use of the same name, the film deals with double identities throughout.

From *La Revue Belge de Cinéma*, no. 11, Spring 1985. © 1985 by Michel Grodent. Reprinted by permission. Translated by Dan Fainaru.

All the characters here have a double, that of the film itself and that of the film within the film.

Q: *The main musical theme is introduced very early in the film.*
A: Indeed. The film director goes down to his studio and turns the radio on, and we hear a Vivaldi-like concerto grosso. This theme will be repeated again and again through the film, soon to be joined by the old man's theme. At the end, both themes are performed on the violin by the character playing the old man. It's like a love call to the old woman that, we are lead to believe, is the director's mother, not only in the film within the film but in real life as well.

Q: *I have read your original script, recently published in Athens. That version indeed specifies the wife of the old man looks very much like the director's mother. But there are differences between the script and the film that you obviously introduced on the set. For example, we were supposed to see Alexander waking up in the middle of the night by rumors from the street outside. He walks out and notices a naked man in a window, high up, about to jump down, waving his arms like a huge sea bird and mumbling strange words. Why did you cut out the scene?*
A: I did shoot the scene but left it out because I felt it toppled the delicate balance between the two levels of fiction in my film, namely the film itself and the film being prepared by my protagonist. The director's side of the story was overshadowing the story of the old man. In any case, the point of the scene is repeated elsewhere in the film, for it is all dominated by this search for the right equilibrium and true inspiration.

Q: *Since the director, Alexander, manipulates the real characters surrounding him in order to create his own fiction, would you say this is first and foremost a film on the creative process in art?*
A: Let's just say it is a film about seeking harmony in every sense of the word, a pretty desperate attempt to find a balance between reality and fiction. This is one of the reasons for the important role of the music in this film. It isn't there just to help establish a certain climate, but as a basic component in the structure of the film.

Q: *In* The Travelling Players, *the class struggle found its echo in the confrontation between the songs. Here the young man's theme is opposed to the old man's theme.*

A: I wouldn't say they are opposed. They are different, yes, but that's all. They are compatible, for as I said before, they are united in the end.

Q: *If we approach* Voyage to Cythera *on a psychological level, could we consider the character played by Katrakis (the old man) as the "sublimated father"?*
A: Compared to other fathers in my earlier films, like *Reconstruction* or *The Travelling Players*, I would say this one is more active, and his son, the director, sublimates his image in order to put distance between them. There are two alternatives for ridding oneself of the Father Image and everything it represents, whether it is the past, our personal history or whatever: you can destroy it either by killing it or by sublimating it to a higher level. In this sense, the final departure of the old couple opens the door for the younger man to accomplish his own journey, mentioned all through the film.

Q: *Would it be correct to interpret the entire film as an attempt to exorcise the past, take leave of it . . .*
A: It exorcises the past but at the same time makes its peace with it. It offers the Greek audience a possibility to face the future without the traumas of the past.

Q: *Alexander, the film director, is obviously an author in search of his characters. For example, the screen tests of the old men, all of them once famous actors, who now repeat, a bit derisively, in front of the camera the same two words: "Ego imé" [It's me].*
A: This is another moment when it is not clear whether we deal with reality or with a dream. It is ambiguous and it is up to the viewer to decide.

Q: *These two words, "Ego imé," are repeated several times through the film, first when the old man comes off the Russian ship and then again, in the village, when his wife comes to find him after he locked himself in the house. It's like an incantation.*
A: Or a kind of magic ritual. Why not?

Q: *Then you would agree there is a link also between the screen tests and the land sale in the village, when the names of the peasants are called and each one answers "paron" [here I am]?*

A: Surely. In both cases, this is a mechanical reply made by persons who are being treated like objects. In one case, they are old actors seeking employment, in the second, villagers who are symbolically selling their identity. The director, both times is an observer who dares not intervene, because he is not quite sure the old man is indeed his father.

Q: *Are there other echoes in your film relating between separate scenes?*
A: Yes. For instance, the gas station we see twice, once by day and once by night, both times from the same angle—an identical travelling of the camera. The gas station is the intermediary between the city and the village. Every time I want to show someone going to the village I just show the Mobil station. My elliptical treatment is the opposite of the one used by Wenders in *Paris, Texas*. He insists on the evidence of the journey both in terms of time and space.

Q: *In your case, the abrupt transfer from one world to another underlines the conflict between your characters.*
A: Yes, that's it.

Q: *To put it differently, the consumer society is confronted by the values and the traditions of the past.*
A: The confrontation is between the real world and the dream world, a world unsullied and still pure which exists only in memory. This is the reason the old man refuses to sell his land. At this point we hear the phrase: "They're doing away with the snow in the sky" which means "they are selling all their memories, the best part of their past."

Q: *There are other indications of this confrontation. In the last scene, there is a noisy group of people invading the café, maybe representing the new generation of pleasure-seeking Greeks, who nevertheless are not completely rid of their memories, to judge by their reaction to authority when they are ordered to keep quiet. Was this your intention?*
A: The significance of this scene is not that pat. When the policemen stops the music, he does not imply anything beyond that. When I wrote the scene, I wanted to portray someone who is bothered by music to such an extent that he has it stopped both times when he enters the café.

Q : *What about the man selling lavender?*
A : I needed the suggestion of a scent that would accompany the film throughout. We hear the old man saying several times "Sapio milo." It has been translated as "rotten apple," but I prefer "withered apple," which not only has an aroma of its own but sounds as an allegory, a metaphor. At one point, the old man says it in Russian, and through the change of language it somehow acquires more weight.

Q : *Should we see it as a political metaphor?*
A : There is always a political interpretation to everything, but one shouldn't overdo it. At this point in the story, the old man is lost, not quite Russian nor Greek, but whatever language he uses, the words are the same: "Rotten apple." The expression crossed my mind accidentally as I was visiting a house while looking for locations. Someone had forgotten on the floor some apples that were slowly rotting away. The aroma was powerful, a kind of friendly, hot, and human fragrance. It is one of those abstract poetic elements spread through film.

Q : *The main theme of the film within the film being shot by the director in* Voyage to Cythera *is the return home of an exile and the various phases he undergoes as he rediscovers his own country after a thirty-two-years-long absence. The difficulty of finding again one's identity, the lack of any physical or emotional point or landmark to lean on. George Seferis [a Greek poet and writer, Nobel Prize for Literature, 1963, D. F.] often dealt with this theme.*
A : The "nostos" is part of our cultural tradition. Homer was already referring to "the journey home"—"Nostimon Imar." For some reason, the Greeks have always been in "diaspora." Greeks, by nature, are travelers, and everywhere they land they start a colony. It's an old story, reflected in the character of the old man as well.

Q : *For you, the old man represents all the Greeks coming home: both emigrants and political exiles.*
A : Exactly. As far as I am concerned, Spyros could have returned after forty years from Australia. Though in our case, there is the political aspect to consider as well. He was a revolutionary who fought the civil war on the side of the communists. But most Greek emigrants returning from work in Germany or elsewhere can easily identify with Spyros's experiences.

Q: *For the Greek audiences, the film offers the additional bonus of several emigrant songs, such as Tsitsanis's "San Apokliros yirizo" ("Coming Back like a Wretch").*

A: There is also a rembetiko composed by Dalaras, using one of the themes of the main Concerto, a song about wandering, solitude, and oblivion. And there is another song, more political, played on the public address system in the harbor, asking everyone to join the dockers' celebrations. That song mentions frozen chimneys, abandoned machinery rusting away, scabs used against strikers ("we'll never give up—better take the road and emigrate"). This is the type of communist song often heard at this kind of festivities.

Q: *And let's not forget Theodorakis's "To traino fevyi stis ochto" ["The Train Leaves at Eight"].*

A: Yes, they are all supposed to create the musical climate of the film.

Q: *In Greece they call it the color of "xenitia" [being abroad]. At a certain point, the old man says a few words which sound like a popular song. ("The first year, OK . . . then the second, then the third . . . you're drifting away, there's nothing to get a grip on. At first, it was Greece and everything you left behind. . . . At the end, you're sick. . . . And then, one day, a woman from that faraway land sews a button on your shirt, washes a piece of your clothing . . . offers you a hot meal . . ."). "Stranger, wash your own linen," says the song.*

A: Beside the notion of the real, physical exile, there is also that of the inner exile, of dispossession. The origin of the film is an old poem I wrote once; I thought I would plant it somewhere in the film, but finally I didn't. It said, among other things: "I wish you health and happiness / But I cannot join you on your journey / I am just a guest / Everything I touch / Makes me really suffer / And it's not mine anyway / There is always someone who will say / It's mine / Me, I have nothing of my own. . . .

Q: *A white ship, gliding like a huge bird over the sea (to use the description in the scenario), brings back the old man to Piraeus. What a magnificent shot. Is it just by chance that the boat's name is* Ukraina?

A: Yes, but we almost shot another Soviet ship, named *Samarkanda*, which is the name of a town that has taken in quite a few political refugees from Greece. The only reason we did not use that boat was its date of arrival, which did not coincide with our schedule.

Q: *The first things we see, when the old man comes off the ship, are his feet.*
A: Because for the time being he is no more than a shadow. Voula, supposedly the film director's sister, says as much when she explains why she did not want to come: "Who cares? Father or not. What does it all mean, anyway, why waste our time chasing a shadow?" We are at the early stages of the fiction within the fiction, the character of the old man is gradually established under our own eyes. For this reason I use a zoom lens, gradually concentrating on him as if drawing his portrait.

Q: *And the old man says: "Ego imé."*
A: Yes, the director has finally found his character.

Q: *There are no embraces when they meet?*
A: It's only normal. They do not know each other. They hesitate, communication is difficult, there is a chill in the air.

Q: *His coming back on a white ship, is this the symbolic return of the inhibited past?*
A: Could be. The scene could be considered as a symbolic emergence of the inhibited past, following the normalization of the political conditions in Greece. But the act of bringing out into the open memories of the resistance and the civil war lacks the impact it might have had several years earlier, when Greece was just coming out of seven years of dictatorship. The only reason the past comes back is to die.

Q: *The beautiful white ship mocks the tragic past; it's almost like a first class funeral. From the very first moment we have the impression the old man is no more than a cumbersome package.*
A: There is fear on both sides. The only thing his wife dares ask this man she hasn't seen for ages is: "Have you eaten?" There is a kind of decent reserve, of humble modesty that prevents all the tenderness welling up inside her from coming out and puts in her mouth other words than those she intended to say. It's almost like closing a door because she could not stand being confronted with his presence. Maybe she feels she has been betrayed.

Q: *All he has to say about Russia is that in winter there is a lot of snow.*
A: It's normal. This man has been deported, his heart full of love for his own country, Greece. What he is trying to express is not his vision of the

other country. He could have said as well: "It's been cold all these years because everything I loved was back home." Though he finally did manage to strike roots there, to marry, to establish a temporary existence, an interval he did not want in his own life but could not escape.

Q: *After confessing to this temporary existence, the old man leaves.*
A: He feels he is a stranger, he can't stay. It's the old woman's house, not his. To connect again with the feelings of old, he has to find a place where they have been happy together, in a hotel near the train station, where they once stayed the night of their trip to Athens. But the old woman does not leave her home, shutting herself inside her kitchen.

Q: *One could say* Voyage to Cythera *is also a dream of love rediscovered?*
A: Of course, the story of Ulysses and Penelope, though I did not want to insist on the analogies.

Q: *Unlike some of your earlier films, where there are abundant references to the myths you use, here the myth is barely suggested. The only clear allusion to the* Odyssey *is the moment when the old man encounters his dog in the village and calls him Argos.*
A: The triangle Ulysses-Penelope-Telemachus represents in this context the end of a journey. If one considers the last forty years in Greece as another War of Troy, the return of Ulysses is the obvious conclusion. It closes the cycle of my earlier films, all of them focusing on the war, since *The Days of '36* and up to *Megalexandros*. The leading figure of previous conflicts, the revolutionary, comes back to a country that rejects revolution and has no use for him. Old Ulysses refuses to accept any compromises; therefore, he does not fit in anymore; there is no role for him to play. He is like a bottle thrown into the sea—a derisive, useless hope to be gotten rid of.

Q: *Does this mean* Voyage to Cythera *is the end of a cycle?*
A: Exactly, it is the epilogue.

Q: *The son, Telemachus in the myth, is called Alexander in your film. Is there a reference to Alexander the Great?*
A: None. The only possible reference to be found is to the little boy Alexander we see leaving for the city at the end of *Megalexandros*. This kind of epi-

logue is essential for the character of the director, heir to a revolutionary tradition, who has to rid himself of the traumas of the past in order to face the present.

Q: *The village you use in* Voyage to Cythera *looks very much like the one in* Megalexandros.
A: True, this is one of the mountain villages in which we shot *Megalexandros*. All those villages were in the hands of the resistance during the war, and people in the underground used to communicate by whistling, just as we see it being done in *Voyage to Cythera*. Whistled languages have been used since the Turkish occupation. Outlaws would warn each other of danger this way. All these remote villages in the mountains, once built for the safety and refuge they offered, have been now abandoned, their inhabitants running away to the valleys, to the cities, or abroad, any place where life conditions are a bit better. But the consumer society is now recuperating the mountains for their secondary residences, turning old villages into ski resorts.

Q: *The old man seems to be the last keeper of an old tradition, a "dancer." I am referring to the sequence of the traditional dance he performs.*
A: Metaphorically, he represents a generation and its attitude to life. He is part of our history, the generation when the great hope that we can change our country was born, a generation that is disappearing with him.

Q: *Many people feel this is a sad film, even pessimistic.*
A: Of course there is sadness, profound regret for all that is irremediably lost. But I believe that in the end, it is neither optimistic nor pessimistic; it is lucid. And this is the only way to advance. Deeply disappointed by the modern world around him, Alexander uses the imaginary journey of the film he makes to free himself from the past.

Q: *When discussing* The Hunters, *you said it was portraying the consciousness of the right wing. Is this film an anatomy of the left?*
A: Let's say a certain kind of left, because not all the left is to be identified with Alexander. I would say this film deals with the state of mind of the modern man who realizes no change is possible before restructuring the ethical and esthetic codes we live by, without taking hold of oneself and one's

memory and putting them in order, without dealing with the obstacles presented by the past.

Q: *Cinema as therapy?*
A: I always say that my films are my universities. I learned a lot from my films. They are my personal luggage and my psychoanalytic sessions.

Q: *Does Alexander represent the end of ideology?*
A: This is rather Voula's role, when she roughly accuses her father of egoism. Voula embodies the conflict of generations: she has been the victim of her father's revolutionary dedication. She has hoped, herself, to change the world but nothing happened and she is bitterly disappointed; there is nothing she believes in any more. In this respect, she is the opposite of her mother, who has gradually found her way back to true love. Voula is even more disgusted than Alexander with the world she lives in. Alexander is still searching for love; she has given up. She uses her body as a last refuge, but her fling with the sailor doesn't offer more than a brief moment of excitement. Nothing more, no sentiment.

Q: *Is the mother the truly strong one?*
A: She is the victim of everything that happened, but she is the only one who remained true to herself all these years. Her almost incredible fidelity to her husband—let me just remind you all this happens in the film within the film—gives her the right to invent once again true love for herself.

Q: *Would this signify that women are no longer marginalized in Greek cinema?*
A: Let me put it this way. Compared with my earlier films, the woman here is more assertive, she no longer accepts following male initiatives.

Q: *Could we say that* Voyage to Cythera *brings you back to classical narrative?*
A: The confusion of ideologies has pushed into the background the different approaches we used to interpret the world. When I began, Marx and Freud were still key figures, just like Hegel and Lenin, and one would naturally use their teachings to observe the world. Let me add that our bitter, very brutal, manichaean experiences in recent Greek history have encouraged us to use dialectics in order to decode all social and esthetic phenomena around us. Briefly, we had the feeling that reality confirms theory, that theory and

practice are coinciding. Since the normalization set in, we are looking for new approaches, and I have the feeling we are coming back to a kind of existentialism. Art is once again anthropocentric and has far more questions than answers. The world is a chessboard on which man is just another pawn and his chance of an impact on the proceedings, negligible. Politics is a cynical game that has turned its back on the commitments of the past. This does not necessarily mean we have to go back to the hero in the primitive sense of the word, but at least to a narrative that puts man in the center. It is not a return to psychology, but a transition from the generalities of the epics to a far more personal cinema, in which the filmmaker is questioning himself and his art.

Q: *Briefly, one could say that we are back to audience identification with the characters?*
A: If I look at my own record, I believe that in my previous films my first concern was a faithful reconstruction, and this concern was so much in evidence, it excluded any type of identification. After a long, difficult period, we return to sentiment. Naturally, *Voyage to Cythera* has the benefit of all the experience I acquired in all these other films. But now, it is no longer the event but the sentiment that dictates the proceedings. I am going much further than ever before into the details of my paintings.

Q: *But this does not exclude the presence of the old Angelopoulos, his alienation and irony. For instance, in the scene of the military taking up positions in the village to search for the old man who had disappeared....*
A: Yes. I wanted to underline the resistance generated by Spyros who refuses to leave the house, partly because he is affected by the violence against him.

Q: *What really happened with these people who came home from exile? Were they forbidden to stay in Greece longer than a certain period of time?*
A: Some were given one month, others maybe three, not more, unless they managed to obtain some legal status. But many exiles, though they had been absent for thirty-five years from Greece, refused to leave again.

Q: *More irony in the sequence of the party taking place in the harbor café. As a matter of fact, there are many parties in your films. Is this an interesting metaphor in your eyes?*

A: No, I suspect it is the Greek habit of partying that inspired me. In Greece, you don't really need a reason to put together a band, some singers, and throw a party. In this case, the dockers' union is celebrating. The irony here is that a PA system is pumping through the speakers all kinds of revolutionary songs in an empty deserted place; obviously no one is interested to join the class struggle. Gone is the enthusiasm that inflamed the masses after the fall of the Colonels. These celebrations and party feasts are nothing more than empty political exercises.

Q: *But when the old woman is invited by the moderator to use the PA system to call her husband, already on the raft at sea, would you call that derision?*
A: No, she knows this is the only way she can reach him and express her love for him.

Q: *It is as if there is no other way for these two persons to talk, except in the context of this festivity.*
A: I wanted to stress, by using this context, the unusual character and the intensity of their relationship. Only in these circumstances could the couple, so clumsy at communicating with each other, find a way to talk.

Q: *What is the role of this downpour which seems to inundate the whole film?*
A: It rains to prevent the festivity. Of course, you can interpret it any way you wish: a metaphor, an allegory, a wish to enforce even more the dramatic situation of the old man, all alone at sea. Let's not forget it is the director, Alexander, who calls all the shots, who picks the sets, creates the atmosphere, decides when it rains and when night falls.

Q: *There is another sequence that has been often discussed—the meeting of the director and his lover.*
A: Here we go back to the first level of the fiction. The film describes one day in the life of the director. It is limited by a certain number of hours. He moves between his house and the film studio. He takes a walk, reflects on his state of mind, everything underlined by the music on the soundtrack. He is greeting everyone as if he is about to undertake a journey. The woman making love in the theatre is his sister, in the film within the film, thus there is a barely indicated suggestion of possible incest. She begs him: "Don't go," but

he goes, nevertheless. He has to pursue his self-probing journey and continue . . . his film.

Q: *What play is being rehearsed on stage?*
A: It is Ibsen's *Hedda Gabler*, at the end of which the heroine commits suicide. I manipulated the end somewhat. In Ibsen the suicide takes place in a room and the characters who discover her are supposed to say: "This is not done." I turned the situation around. It is a play about lost illusions, and therefore a perfect illustration of my theme.

Q: *Once again, your predilection for "the play within a play."*
A: It is a subterfuge I use again at the end of the film, when we hear, through the loudspeakers, a voice saying "one, two, one, two . . . , one, two, three, four . . ." as if testing the PA system. It is my own voice. Also, I was naughty enough to use the Italian accent Giulio Brogi has, when he speaks a few lines in Greek. For Greeks, his accent is easily noticeable. Once again the game of reality and fiction.

Q: *It is like a kind of counterpoint technique: two stories, a main and a secondary one, the second sometimes supporting, sometimes contrasting the first.*
A: True. It is supposed to suggest the film can be read on several levels, as a realistic story but also as a surreal one (i.e. the sequence of the old man whistling in the fog), without ever becoming a dreamplay. Also that reality, sometimes, is even stranger than fiction. Manos Katrakis, the actor I chose to play the old man because of his physical and moral identification with Spyros, died after the shoot was over. Just like the character he plays, he had survived the revolution, had gone to prison for his politics. I felt somehow he was looking for the right place to die and the film provided him with just that. Strangely enough, the actor who plays his rival in the film died at about the same time. In real life, he belonged to the opposite political party. It is as if the two faces of the past were indeed disappearing at the same time.

Q: *Why does the old man speak of a "third exile"?*
A: The first is the 1922 catastrophe, following the Greek defeat at the hands of Mustafa Kemal (the sick old lady refers to it in the film). The second exile was the one after the civil war. The third is being described by this film,

portraying death slowly approaching, this "call for silence" played by the trumpet in the midst of the main musical theme.

Q: *Why call the film* Voyage to Cythera?
A: Cythera is the island glorified by poets, the island of love, the island of Aphrodite. The title has to reflect the full spirit of the film. In the past, I think I managed to do this pretty well: *The Days of '36* was inspired by Cavafy (*Days of 1909*, etc.). *Megalexandros* refers to the popular tradition of travelling peddlers and shadow shows.

Q: *If you had to pick a poem that would express the sentiments you poured into your film, which one would you choose?*
A: "The Old Man by the River" by Seferis. "All I want is to speak plainly, / may this gift be bestowed upon me. . . ."

Talking about *The Beekeeper*

MICHEL CIMENT/1987

Q: *Your previous film,* Voyage to Cythera, *clearly indicated your disenchantment with the world of politics and, if it did not spell out the death of ideologies in so many words, it certainly provided a point of view on these matters, that was different from all your previous films. Now, in* The Beekeeper *the only reference to politics is in the meeting between Mastroianni and Reggiani, when they talk about old comrades and about missing "their appointment with history." The rest of the film concentrates on the fate and personal problems of one single individual.*

A: Please keep in mind we're talking about a man who is fifty-five years old and carries half a century of history on his back. He is no innocent, he feels the weight of the past on his shoulders. He may mention his former hopes of changing the world, while reminiscing about things gone by in the company of old friends, but this context of the film is clear from the very beginning. He has lived through forty years of intense history, a period of major changes and importance for Greece and the rest of the world. War, repression, but also hope. He is a man of our time, with all this past behind him, facing a young girl who has no memory at all and who calls him "Mister-I-remember." It is the conflict between memory and non-memory. I was often asked: "Why does he commit suicide?" I do not believe he commits suicide. His is an act of despair, but while he is doing it, as he is turning over the beehive, he tries to establish some kind of communication, hitting the ground with his hand the way prisoners do in jail. For he is a prisoner of

---

From *Positif*, no. 315, May 1987. © 1987 by Positif. Reprinted by permission of Michel Ciment. Translated by Dan Fainaru.

certain circumstances, and he tries to communicate with the past. But we have to look for something else. We are now living a major historical moment, waiting for the world to change but having no idea how and when this is going to happen. In any case, it is clear that something has to happen to pull us out of the state we are in. There have always been big, wide gaps in the history of mankind, moments of profound silence. We are living through such a period and this silence can induce terror.

Q : *In your last two films,* Voyage to Cythera *and* The Beekeeper, *you call your hero Spyros. Does it have a particular significance in your eyes?*
A : Spyros was the name of my father. For me, it represents his entire generation. In the context of the films it does not have any significance, but I am very much attached to it. The other thing is that since every one of my films carries the seed for the next one, this is one of the ties between *Voyage to Cythera* and *The Beekeeper*. The choice of the name may also reflect a personal problem—it is quite possible that I am not capable of telling anyone else's stories but my own. Maybe I am simply limited to my own experience, my traumas and my hopes, my own personal growth and evolution. This is why I believe that my next film will come out of *The Beekeeper*.

Q : *You claim the name of your father, which you have given to the character played by Mastroianni, has no particular significance, but paternity seems to be a main theme in your last three films. In* Megalexandros *it was the ideological father, in* Voyage to Cythera *it was biological paternity, and in* The Beekeeper *it is the paternity chosen by the young girl.*
A : It is through the search for the father figure that we seek our way into the future and preserve our emotional balance. The reference to the end of a certain historical period and of the ideals that kept our hopes alive carries with it a sense of frustration, as if being deprived of one's roots. This political unease has its reverberations in one's psyche. The search for a father figure comes out of the need to restore emotional harmony and to feel that one's existence is not just a matter of chance. It is a way of establishing a link between yesterday and tomorrow. In *The Beekeeper* the main character is the father of his own biological daughter but also of the young girl who travels with him. Through both of them, he tries to find a means of reaching into the future. He senses there is an abyss there, more than just a generation gap. It is more like a language gap. Even physical love cannot help him establish

contact with this other generation. Therefore, his intense despair. He leaves the North and heads South, to his hometown, because of the harmony he had experienced there. But what he finds there is just a vale of tears, everything has been destroyed including the cinema. Cinema was once an integral part of our life, part of this world that has collapsed under our eyes. It was one of the means for keeping in contact with life around us and it was one of our creative options.

Q: *Why did you choose a beekeeper for your protagonist?*
A: It is a strange profession. Beekeepers have the soul of poets. They have a privileged relation with nature, and picking honey is like an artistic activity. They communicate with the bees through their senses, and my protagonist falls apart when this communication is interrupted. His final act is directed against the bees as well, like a dying sculptor destroying one of his own statues. While shooting *Travelling Players,* I met a beekeeper who lives on an island and who has become my friend. He played a small part in the film and was the middleman between the local peasants and us. He played again in *Megalexandros* as one of the bandits. To do it he had to leave behind his home and his bees. I like him very much. I often visit him, and every time I am there, I can't help noticing the way he watches his beehives, following the constant traffic of the bees, in and out of the beehive. For him it was an absorbing occupation; he was as attentive as a sound engineer in a recording session. Most of the people who do physical work hate their jobs, because they are usually exhausting and dirty and don't really pay. But beekeepers love their profession; they have an erotic relation with the bees. Therefore, in a way, they are just like artists.

Q: *How can you explain your insistence on making films in the north of Greece?*
A: I don't know. I wonder sometimes why this landscape in the rain and mist, this sadness of the north, is so essential for me. To be quite honest, I have to confess I don't like Paris much in the sunshine either—I prefer it when it's raining.

Q: *Your choice is a bit like Antonioni's predilection for the Po Valley.*
A: Maybe there is something in it. These landscapes have stayed with me from the very first day I started to make films.

Q: *In* The Beekeeper *you use locations that have served you before in previous films. For instance, Iannina.*
A: Yes, it is true. The two lovers in *Reconstruction* meet at the inn in Iannina. I went there again for *The Travelling Players,* and Iannina with the lake next to it, are featured in *The Hunters* as well. Strange, for I am a southerner through and through. I was born in Athens, the origins of my family are Crete and the Peloponesus and this is indeed the Deep South. And yet, it is a fact, I shot most of my films in the north, particularly in Epirus, a region in northwest Greece. Beyond the rain and the bare landscape, I am particularly fond of the stones and the stone houses. I must be trying to bring up some hidden image from my subconscious, but what image, I don't know.

Q: *You also used a town called Egio.*
A: Yes, for the cinema sequence. Egio is in the Peloponesus, the South of Greece, for this film is crossing the country, starting from Florina, in Macedonia, next to the Albanian and Yugoslav borders in the North and going all the way down South. I shot some scenes in Galaxii and Oumenissa in the North, also in Naphplion, which I also used for *Travelling Players* and *The Hunters,* and of course there are scenes in Athens.

Q: *Did you ever consider the option of working in a film studio?*
A: Never. I feel the need to transform a natural landscape into an internal landscape that I see in my imagination. I have houses repainted, sometimes even relocated; I build bridges that haven't been there before. We even built that space next to the highway for the girl to dance in. All my films are elaborations based on reality. It is not the real landscape I am trying to show, but the one I see in my dreams.

Q: *But given your very complicated sequence shots, for instance the sequence of the bar in which we see the girl dancing, it would be much easier to do that in a studio.*
A: Possibly, but in this case I couldn't move from exterior to interior—to do it I would have to cut. But quite often I need to move inside or out within the same shot. On top of which, let's face it, there isn't much of studio tradition in Greek filmmaking; therefore it is rather risky to do it. Finally, I need a solid realistic basis for my sets before I change it to suit my own needs.

Q: *You've had a very close relationship with your director of photography Giorgos Arvanitis and with your set designer Mikes Karapiperis, who have been working with you since your first film.*
A: We always go out together, the three of us, to look for locations. We discuss the options we have, what should be done to the place to fit it into our plans. Arvanitis checks the color patterns, his lighting options, and the free space for the camera to move in. Once we reach the shoot, most of the work is already done. I believe this is the usual procedure for most films, but since we have known each other for such a long time, we reach our conclusions very quickly. I suppose that in a studio we could move the walls and feel more at ease for the movement of the camera. But then I have no qualms tearing down a real wall, if I think it is really necessary. In any case, I doubt I could feel comfortable in a studio.

Q: *What lenses do you use?*
A: This time, I used several lenses, even a zoom. I did it not because I needed the zoom effect but because I needed to change the space relations between the actor, the landscape, and the camera. But basically, I always use a 35 mm, sometimes 40 mm, going up—very rarely—to 80 mm. I find the 35 particularly satisfying because it is quite wide without distorting the image. It is the closest to the human eye. Maybe less than the 40, but it has the depth of focus which I find essential. In this film, I wanted to control in particular the distances between the man and the woman. Showing them closer or farther apart, is a way of reflecting on the distance separating their respective worlds. In the hotel room, for instance, I never wanted them to share the same frame; I wanted the camera to move from one to the other.

Q: *While Spyros seems to be on a journey back to the earth, the bird in the first sequence of the film and the bees, of course, express the wish to fly.*
A: To begin with, I feared the bird would be taken for some kind of symbol, which was not my intention. I just wanted to create a sense of unease in the relations of the married couple. For a symbol, I would have had the bird hit a blank wall.

Q: *How about the song "I went up into the pear tree"?*
A: It's one of those tunes I heard all through my childhood. I was brought up with it, just like my daughters are today. It's a surrealist song—a pear tree

is too small to climb on. "And then I cut my hand." I have no idea what this line is supposed to mean.

Q: *Still, you used it for the film's ending!*
A: Yes, but it was not my intention to underline it. Mastroianni is singing this ditty to his daughter, the same one he was singing to her when she was a baby.

Q: *The Serge Reggiani sequence is the only one which refers to the past.*
A: We know that Spyros used to be a school teacher who left his job. It is clear, from the very beginning of the film, that he is taking his leave from everything and everybody. It is only normal that he should say good bye to old friends. This sequence is the only moment when we understand that he has had his own role to play in his country's history. It's a kind of reference to *Voyage to Cythera*, the difference there being that the old man there comes back from exile, Ulysses returning home. In *The Beekeeper* the protagonist did not leave his homeland. It is the logical sequel to the previous film and at the same time, it completes a cycle. It is also the first time that, at the end of a film, I have no project in sight for the next. I feel I need to wait, bide my time and think carefully. I think I am on the brink of starting a new cycle, one that can no longer be based on memory. I suspect I exhausted the history of my generation. Maybe I should try to talk about the younger generation, about the young girl in *The Beekeeper*, about the present and the future in store for them. There are as many reasons today to go on living, as there are for dying.

Q: *You are part of a generation which has excelled in its political portraits of your time, people like Rosi, the Taviani brothers, Denys Arcand, all of whom are now focusing on personal rather than historical portraits.*
A: Probably because history is now silent. And we are all trying to find answers by digging into ourselves, for it is terribly difficult to live in silence. When there is no historical development, one is tempted to focus on oneself, in the context of this crisis that has interrupted the historical continuity. For our generation, having taken an active part in keeping this continuity alive, this is very sad, the kind of disappointment that is very difficult to express.

Q: *Because of the titles, many people felt* Travelling Players *was related in some way to* Voyage to Cythera, *but if there is a companion piece for it, it should be* The Beekeeper.

A: Yes, for this is the beekeeper's voyage. A personal trip that in some way replaces the collective journey of the travelling players.

Landscape in the Mist

SERGE TOUBIANA AND FRÉDÉRIC STRAUSS / 1988

Q: *The "landscape" in the title of your new film seems to carry a particular significance. One could consider the two children who are the protagonists of the films to be a kind of landscape which you observe as if you were watching from a distance a place that is not familiar but you would like to get acquainted with.*

A: Yes, it's what I refer to as human geography. It often happens when you look at a film where you feel you know everything there is to know about the physical aspect of the persons on screen and there is nothing more for you to find out about them. *Landscape in the Mist* is a kind of fairytale in which I was trying to preserve the delight and wonder of an initial discovery.

Q: *The point of view you choose and the distance you keep between the camera and your protagonists prevent the immediate identification of the audience with the children. There are few commercial gimmicks more obvious than the use of children, but you manage, in a masterful way, to drain almost all pathos out of their performance.*

A: I was not attempting to exploit either the natural photogenic appeal or the inevitable pathos children usually evoke. Differently shot and putting these qualities in evidence, this could have been a tremendous commercial hit. I was very conscious of this risk, but on the other hand, I did not want to empty their roles of all the emotion. I had to find the right balance between the two. I had already attempted, in *The Beekeeper*, to reach the limits

From *Les Cahiers du Cinéma*, no. 413. © 1988 by Cahiers du Cinéma. Reprinted by permission. Translated by Dan Fainaru.

of non-expressive acting with Mastroianni, whose personality is far too well known to generate the kind of surprise I was referring to before. It was my way of discovering something different in him. I never used a close-up on him in his emotional scenes. I always fear those frames that practically scream, "Look at me!" For this reason I like Antonioni and the early Wenders, films like *Alice in the Cities* more than *Wings of Desire*, though I think his recent work is interesting.

Q: *How did you work with the children?*
A: The boy, Michalis Zeke, was five and a half years old when we shot the film. I felt that the best way to communicate with him was to convince him that he was participating in a game. When we were rehearsing the scene where he sees the horse dying and bursts into tears, he came to me and said, "Mr. Angelopoulos, I am terribly annoyed but I cannot cry. I am very sad but I cannot do it." I told him: "Listen, you must cry in this scene. Feeling sad inside is not enough, you have to show it to the audience." He reflected for a minute and then proposed: "You know what? You scold me; this will make me cry and we'll shoot the scene." We tried but it didn't work, so we went back to the hotel and there I went through the scene with him once more, in a much rougher way than before. The crew was all around us. He felt humiliated, turned his back on me, and started to cry. I took him by the hand, we went back to the set and did the scene in one take. While for him everything was a game, the girl, Tania Palaiologlou, who was much older, required a different type of treatment. She was going through that very difficult period between childhood and adolescence. As a matter of fact, she first menstruated on the set, and she fell in love with Stratos Tzortzolglou, the actor who plays Orestes. Since it was in the spirit of the film, I did not interfere. Her real problem, however, was the rape scene, which she refused to do, despite all my entreatings, for I felt I needed it in the film. She would shut herself up in her room and would not discuss it at all. She finally agreed to play the scene but refused to scream when the truck driver pulls her with him, as the script had her do. It was her own idea to play it like that and I found that it suited the film perfectly. For her, I used a sentimental, emotional approach rather than a confrontational one. The only game she played was the "silence game." While the crew was setting up the lights, we, that is the kids, Orestes, and me, would try to see who could be silent for half an hour or more until the lights were set. Sometimes, to ease the silence, I

would play music from the film. I was amazed to see these two children who would not open the mouth for such a long time, knowing from my personal experience with my own daughters, who are more or less the same age, how difficult it is for them not to speak for so long. These moments of silence were a great help with the mood of the film.

Q: *Are you trying to tell us that the director is an actor as well?*
A: Certainly. I do not believe the director should play the scenes for the actor to imitate, but without asking him to ape the model, you can suggest the kind of acting you want by creating certain moods. When I first started making films, I didn't like professional actors much. Their performance seemed false to me. I preferred to work with non-professionals, but I found out that they aren't always sensitive to the pace of the scene and they tend to overplay the dramatic moments. Mastroianni once told me something I like very much: "I am the child and you are the parent telling me stories. If you know how to tell them well, I will play your game."

Q: *Isn't this one way of describing the role of the moving pictures, the relation between the filmmaker and the audience?*
A: Yes, it is. Mastroianni claims he can not understand the actors who expect to be told everything about the characters they play before they start the picture and require logical explanations for everything they do in it. He let himself go, allowed himself to be carried away by the flow of the story.

Q: *Is the process of writing a very long one for you? And when it is finished, do you actually have a shooting script in your hands?*
A: No, as a matter of fact my scenarios are not real scripts. Often they look more like a novel—though unlike the normal literary novel, you won't find in them one single adjective. If, for instance, there is a handsome boy in the story, I delete the term "handsome" to prevent a set image of the character entering too soon into the picture. On the other hand, I often specify the presence of sound effects, such as birds singing. This happened when I wrote *Landscape in the Mist*. It was at a very early stage I put it in the script, long before I had any idea about the music which comes much later. The flight of the two children in this film recalls romantic adventures from yesteryear; therefore when I thought about music, it was in the terms of Cesar Frank and Mendelssohn. Once I decide on the type of music I would like to have, there

is the choice of the best instrument suitable for this music, and in this case, I felt the oboe would be the right choice, somewhere between sweet romanticism and a cry of pain. Then I read the scenario as if it was a story and try to imagine the colors associated with it, without considering any of the script's specifications. For the scene where everyone stops to watch the falling snow, we asked the city employees to come out in their yellow parkas. I thought it would be a good idea to use this pattern of colors again, and in the train station sequence, we see the railwaymen walking by on the rails, dressed in yellow. These are the types of improvisations done on the spot, while shooting; it is not something you plan beforehand. I went through the IDHEC and there we were taught to be faithful to the script in every detail, the great Hitchcock tradition. Personally, I believe there is a large margin of creativity available to be found between the Hitchcock tradition and the Godardian school. The selection of the right location is of major importance for me. I always shoot on location but I always change it around to suit my needs. The only thing that is not changed is the sense of the scene, but I can treat it in various manners.

Q : *The symbolic images in your film, are they already in the script?*
A : Yes. The piece of film found by Orestes was in the script, but, for technical reasons, we could not follow it all the way through. I intended to have the camera approach this single image and actually enter it. For this, we had to prepare two inter-negatives and the image lost its definition. What is left in the film, is only half of the idea I had. For me, the symbolic elements are a means of escaping the confines of the simple narrative, explorations of a surreal world. They are inserted into the fabric of the script, though quite often I am not sure what they mean. For instance, I couldn't really tell you the significance of the stone hand pulled out of the Thessaloniki harbor. The basic structure of this film, as I told you, was similar to a fairytale, which gives you much greater freedom to introduce elements that are outside the logic of the plot. But one should not try to systematically unravel their meanings, for you risk losing the flow of the narrative. There is a hint of homosexuality in the scene when Orestes is selling his motorcycle to another young man. Tonino Guerra, who worked with me on the script, wanted to know the purpose of this hint. I didn't have an answer—all I knew was that it felt right.

Q: *This scene has something to do with fetishism.*
A: Well, we know there is an erotic attraction between a man and his motorcycle. I did not pay the actor; instead I gave him the bike and you cannot imagine his joy. It was almost embarrassing.

Q: *The most important thing in your films seems to be the consistence of every single shot. It has to have its own force and build up its intensity as it goes.*
A: It is for this reason that my personal film language is based on expanding the dimension of time. Before you enter into the gist of any given shot, you have to be given the time to find out the relations between the actor and the landscape. For this reason, I love Tarkovsky's *Stalker; Nostalghia,* I like less; *Sacrifice,* I do not like at all. As far as I am concerned, the Holy Trinity—that of the actor, the landscape, and the camera—is perfect in *Stalker.*

Q: *In most of your films, there seems to be a sense of melancholy for the past. But the two children, who are not subject to this melancholy, are pulling you in a different direction.*
A: I believe the past is my own personal past dragged into the present by my occupation as a filmmaker. The tree at the end of the film is the tree from *Voyage to Cythera,* a reference to my own personal film landscape. In the course of this picture, the children cross a film landscape in order to reach, at the end, a different film landscape, which, I believe, should offer them renewed hope. I would like to believe the world will be saved by the cinema. Cinema is my world and it is the scope of all my journeys. I am always searching for secret little utopias that will enchant me; I am doing my best to believe in the relevance of these trips I am constantly embarking on through my films.

Q: *Isn't this melancholic attitude to the past related to the present state of cinema and your perception of it?*
A: The cinema crisis does not refer only to the decrease in the number of admissions. In the seventies, filmmakers were still looking for new horizons. Now it's over. Despite a few good films, the general impression is that movies are out of breath. For us, the cinema was a bit like the crusades, going out to save the world. Today, young directors are working with the same technical crews I use. This requires a lot of money and the higher the cost, the narrower becomes the margin for adventurous explorations. I was talking to

Michalis Fotopoulos as Costas and Toula Stathopoulou as Eleni in *Reconstruction (Anaparastasi)*, 1970

Days of '36 (Meres Tou '36), 1972

The Travelling Players (O Thiassos), 1975

The Hunters (I Kynighi), 1977

Omero Antonutti (left) as Megalexandros in *Alexander the Great (Megalexandros)*, 1980

Dora Volanaki as Katerina and Manos Katrakis as Old Man Spyros in *Voyage to Cythera (Taxidi Sta Kythira)*, 1983

Marcello Mastroianni as Spyros and Nadia Mourouzi as the young girl in *The Beekeeper (O Melissokomos)*, 1986

Tania Palaiologlou as Voula, Stratos Tzortzoglou as Orestes, and Michalis Zeke as Alexander in *Landscape in the Mist (Topio Stin Omichli)*, 1988

Gregory Karr as the journalist and Ilias Logothetis as the colonel in *The Suspended Step of the Stork (To Meteoro Vima Tou Pelargou)*, 1991

Harvey Keitel as A in *Ulysses' Gaze (To Vlema Tou Odyssea)*, 1995

Fabrizio Bentivoglio (right) as Solomos in *Eternity and a Day (Mia Eoniotita Ke Mia Mera)*, 1998

Oshima some time ago, and we both shared the feeling that our generation was more politically committed, and that when we were young, we sincerely believed things are really going to change. Now, all this is obviously over.

Q: *The feeling of nostalgia in your films is probably generated also by the fact that they do not seem to have a clear-cut ending; they could go anywhere and the spectator is given the freedom to speculate on it.*
A: There is no end in my films. I have the feeling that everything around me stands still. I am trying to break away from this immobility, to break new ground, but there is nothing very stimulating happening around me. Oshima told me the same thing, when I asked him why he is not shooting in Japan any more. Nothing stimulates him there, he said.

Angelopoulos's Philosophy of Film

GERALD O'GRADY/1990

THEO ANGELOPOULOS RESPONDED IN Greek to my questions while in his Athens office on Sunday afternoon September 2. George Kaloyeropoulos of the Greek Film Center acted as the intermediary and later transcribed the responses. These were translated by Steve Dandolos and Stefanos Papazacharias.

Q: *You have now made eight major features over a twenty-year period, and your films are well known and have received many awards throughout all the countries in Europe and Japan. But, here in the United States, only a very few have ever been shown and then only sporadically, before your complete retrospective at The Museum of Modern Art in February. And it is only this month that two of your films, one made fifteen years ago and the other your most recent, are finally being put into commercial distribution. Despite the international consensus that you rank with such masters as Antonioni, Mizoguchi, and Tarkovsky, your work is almost completely unknown to the American audience, including its film critics and its academics. Our first task, it seems to me, is to indicate how different your approach to the cinema is from our American model, though I know that you, on the other hand, are very familiar with all of our popular genres and directors from the 1940s to the present. What I would be most interested in is a descriptive account of your impulses and methods in comparison with those of a typical American director. You might, I hope, talk about why, over a six-year period, you made three films, Days*

Abridged version published in *The Buffalo News*, Sept. 16, 1990. © 1990 by Gerald O'Grady. Reprinted by permission.

of '36, The Travelling Players, *and* The Hunters, *which explore the twenty years of Greek political history starting with your birth. No American does that kind of thing. Just to take Mike Nichols as an example, he first made a film based on Edward Albee's play,* Who's Afraid of Virginia Woolf? *and then one based on Joseph Heller's novel,* Catch-22, *and then* The Day of the Dolphin. *Could you help us prepare our audience for your kind of work?*

A : First of all I don't think anyone could say with absolute certainty that there is a clear distinction between American and European cinema. But in any case, during the first years after the liberation, from '44 on, the American cinema was the only kind available in Greece, and therefore this was the first cinema my generation could see. I know that older directors such as Antonioni, Fellini, or Visconti were influenced more by the French than the American cinema or maybe I should say they began their careers having knowledge of both.

In any case, the impact of the American cinema was felt in Europe for the first time after the war. Its tendencies for detective stories, musicals, social drama, and melodrama and its use of a certain type of narrative to tell these stories were very much favored by mass audiences. As such, it influenced the first postwar generation, namely my own, perhaps the generation after mine and possibly the next one as well. When, by the end of the fifties, the New Wave exploded in France, it represented for people like myself the discovery of another option.

The film that really moved me was Godard's *Breathless*, a detective story in disguise, written in a completely different manner. There is a tremendous disparity in writing between John Huston's classic detective stories and Godard's, but for us, Godard offered the appropriate stimulus by revealing another type of discourse. Of course he was not absolutely original and his option was not the only one. Before him there was the Italian neo-realism and a different approach to writing as it relates to "timing," in the films of Antonioni. In addition, for those of us who managed to follow it, there was also the Japanese cinema. All these kinds of cinema revealed for us a variety of alternatives for writing films and for film making in general. Without realizing it, I found myself making certain choices, though I must say that my initial intellectual experience derived from literature. Therefore, I was prepared for a completely different discourse, as far as texts are concerned. I read mainly the great European writers, but also the Americans we knew so well in Greece, from Whitman to Hemingway, Steinbeck, Faulkner, and Dos

Passos. It is interesting that historically American writers have been always trying to relate to the Europeans. But this did not happen in cinema. European and American literature are much closer related than the European and American cinema.

Of course, Greek literature and specifically Greek tragedy, which represents my first encounter with theater, had an enormous influence on me. Trying to make my own choices in light of all these experiences, I soon reached the conclusion that the story and its writing process are of equal importance. By the way, many times the process of writing ends up becoming the story of the film. Therefore, not only the stories I narrate but also the way in which I narrate them are equally important to me.

Being born shortly before WW2, I could not avoid being marked by history, particularly that of my own country. The dictatorship before the war, then the war and everything that happened after it: the civil war and then another dictatorship. It would have been impossible for me to escape from my own life and experience. In my attempt to understand I make films based on history or reflections on history. It is only natural for me to delve into my own past in order to define my own story within the history of a place. During the '67–'74 dictatorship in Greece I suddenly underwent this shock. Everything I had experienced as a young boy with my father, his being jailed and later sentenced to death, and a lot of other things, all these events came back to me and became the material to review my personal history in the context of my country's history.

Q: *Our audience is quite familiar with the work, for example, of Ingmar Bergman, who, like yourself, writes all of his own scripts. But while you use, just like him, a regular cameraman, in your case Giorgos Arvanitis, for all your films, and you also have the tendency to work with the same ensemble of actors and actresses, I sense there is a major difference between the two of you. He seems to write his scripts with his performers in mind, but you don't. Also, while his fictions express his own personal psychic stresses, even neuroses (and I don't mean that in a critical way), your work centers more on the contemporary political history of your own country and is also mediated through your own cultural history, Homer, Aeschylus, Euripides and Sophocles, and Alexander the Great. I think it might be useful if you would define your* modus operandi *in relation to Bergman's, so that we can use the known to prepare us for the unknown.*

A: I don't find any similarities between my work and Bergman's. My cinema is not psychological, it is epic; the individual in it is not psychoanalyzed but placed within a historical context. My characters assume all the elements of epic cinema or, if I may say so, those of epic poetry, typically featuring clear-cut persona. In Homer, Odysseus is a shrewd conniver, Achilles is brave, loyal to his friends—and these characteristics never change. The same with Brecht whose characters are larger than life; they serve as carriers of history or ideas. My characters are not being analyzed, they are not tormented, like Bergman's. They are more humane. They search for lost things, all that was lost in the rupture between desire and reality. Until not very long ago the history of the world was based on desire; the desire to change the world one way or another. Now at the end of the century we realize that whatever was desired never really happened, and it did not happen for reasons that I am unable to explain. Perhaps it was impossible to change things using the specific methods that were employed at the time, but in any case, we are left with the experience of our failure, with the ashes of the disappointment of dreams that never materialized. My last three films reflect this taste of ashes, leaving the desire to be pursued in some future time, in the next discourse. My writing and Bergman's do not relate. In his films there is a strong metaphysical element which identifies the search for the father figure with the search for God or the denial of God. I think that in my own work, the father figure does not represent a goal in itself; the purpose of my films is to find a reason to exist. My films are not as metaphysical. They are, in a strange way, more existential than Bergman's. This is certainly the case for the trilogy *Voyage to Cythera, The Beekeeper,* and *Landscape in the Mist.*

Q: *In between your historical trilogy,* Days of '36, Travelling Players, *and* The Hunters, *and the second one, there is* Megalexandros. *While still partially based on actual history, an event which took place in 1870 when a group of English tourists was kidnapped by Greek bandits from Marathon, it is largely concerned with elements of the fantastic, even the surrealistic. It retells a popular legend that derives from the fifteenth century, about a country waiting for a liberator, a sort of messiah, but once he emerges, he turns into a tyrant. At the same time, the film seems to be an allegorical meditation on modern dictators. Is this really the pursuit of history by other means, and is this tension between realism and surrealism more central to your work than it first appears to be?*

A: *Megalexandros* is a philosophical-political reflection on power, on the problems of authority, and as such it represents the bitter end result of my previous three films. Whatever could be identified as human hope in my earlier work tends to shrink in this one, dissolved as if from within, and this is tragic. *Megalexandros* addressed the concentration of power long before the changes in Eastern Europe took place, and in this respect it was a prophetic film on the failure of the socialist experiment in this part of the world. I could not have spelled it out in any other way at the time. I had to use the form of a myth. I did not want to make use of authentic facts because it would have imposed a departure from a poetic language, and I believe that a film must be, before anything else, a poetic event, otherwise it does not exist. This is true for the work of directors I admire, like Oshima and the Tavianis, who are using similar methods, going back into the past in order to speak about the present.

Q: *It seems to me that, more than any other director on the world scene, your characters inhabit not only a distinct* place, *but also a distinct* time. *There is no question but that your screen vibrates with a physical presence of Greece—the stones, the streets, the walls, the roofs, the skies, the rain, the fog. You have few, if any, peers in conveying this sense of place. But I think your feeling for time, for history, is what makes you different. Your first film,* Reconstruction, *is a reenactment of a real murder, based on newspaper accounts and court records; the historical trilogy speaks for itself; and even Spyros, as he travels from the north to the south of Greece in* The Beekeeper, *remembers, in almost cinéma-verité-like flashbacks, scenes of his earlier life. You really bind the mind to actuality, to history, even if you acknowledge that it is a reconstruction, and, of course, you continually refer your characters to heroes in earlier Greek history, through allusions to the classics, mentioned above. How do you explain this acute sense of history, this "documentary" thrust in your films?*

A: I wouldn't call this sense of history "a documentary thrust." I rather think it is a Greek tradition. If we recall the Greek classics, we notice that most of them work with myths referring to much older periods, and in this context history is used as a continuous backdrop, independent of any thematic concerns. My attachment to our history derives from the fact that I am Greek, from the overall relationship of history with Greek art and specifically with literature, and in this century, with Greek cinema. For many years, in my country, no unconventional approach to history was conceivable; the general consensus was the only acceptable attitude. But after the collapse of the dictatorship in 1974, there was a real explosion in Greece in terms of historical-political films. These films should have been done years ago. I am not referring, of course, to my own films, because I was exploring this territory already during the dictatorship. I mean the Greek cinema in general, which started discussing these things only after they were gone, and by then it was too late. At the same time, one has to concede that the Greek cinema, due to lack of resources, was dependent on comedies or star-studded tearjerkers, thus bringing forward mostly farces and melodramas for domestic consumption. Once in a while, there was a film that contained elements of real tragedy, like Cacoyannis's *Stella, Drakos* by Kondouros, based on folklore, or *Paranomi,* by the same Kondouros, based on history.

If we are to speak about time, we must divide it into historical time and "timing." Usually, a move in time is achieved through flashbacks, through a cut that never attempts to manipulate historical time. In an old American film by Laszlo Benendek the movement from present to past takes place within the same space through a simple change in lighting. In a Swedish film, *Miss Julie,* time moves through the personal reminiscences of the characters; in other words, every time one of them recollects something from the past, we are taken back to it. What I did was something that was achieved for the first time in the history of cinema. My own work is based on what we call collective memory, and more than collective individual memory, on collective historical memory, mixing time in the same space, changing time not through a flashback that corresponds to a person but to a collective memory, and this was accomplished without a cut. The change was made within the same shot in such a way that three or four different historical periods coexist in the space of this shot, a series of frightening leaps into time. For example, in *The Travelling Players* an actor is talking about Asia Minor while the train is travelling in the year 1940, the beginning of the war. When the train stops, the actor gets off and looking straight into the camera he goes on talking about the war in Asia Minor that happened in 1922. But when he looks into the camera saying all these things, that moment is now, now being each time one sees the film. In this manner three different historical times are being juxtaposed, the present, 1940, and 1922. In another scene, the new cast of the "travelling players" are seen walking down a street in the year 1952 until they vanish, and in that moment the shot becomes panoramic and we see a German vintage car entering the same shot in 1942. As the camera refocuses on the spot where the travelling players had vanished, we now see German soldiers, as the shot is pursued without any interruption. This becomes a continuous, dialectic presentation of different historical moments, but at the same time preventing any factual relationship between them. Therefore, while watching this scene, a second emotion, provided by the cinema language, is added to the initial one. I mean that in the way I use time, time becomes space and space, in a strange way, becomes time. I don't know if what I say makes sense, but there exists an accordion of time and space, a continuous accordion that lends a different dimension to the events being shown on the screen.

Q: *Let's try to discuss now what has become one of the defining visual characteristics of your work, the long take, the tracking shot, the 360 circular shot, all strategies to allow or "make" the viewer "really" see the shot and its specific duration. How did you hit upon it, what is your purpose, does it have anything to do with space or time, or their interaction? Is this at all related to the fact that some of your films are particularly long, and with your choice of placing contemporary characters in the context of the cultural history of your country?*

A: The characteristics of my own work derive, first of all, from my many years of viewing cinema. For years, I watched every type of film around me and absorbed things I found interesting, and when, later on, I attempted to write and to make films, it all came back to the surface and became style, writing, personal writing. If I have to explain this, I would say that my preference for the long shot, the sequence shot, stems from my rejection of what is generally referred to as parallel editing, for I consider it fabricated. For historical reasons I accept the work of all those who resorted to this type of montage, like Eisenstein, but this is not my kind of cinema. In a certain manner, for me, each shot is a living thing, with a breath of its own, that consists of inhaling and exhaling. This is a process that cannot accept any interference; it must have a natural opening and fading.

In today's cinema, the so-called dead time—silence and pauses—has become obsolete. This undefined time that functions between one act and another has disappeared. For me, even silence needs to function in an almost musical way, not to be fabricated through cuts or through dead shots but to exist internally inside the shot. I have used fast and slow internal rhythms in the long shot in order to project a ceremonial element. *Megalexandros* is structured like a Byzantine liturgy containing this ceremonial element in the form of a theatrical gesture that needs to be completed in a specific timing. The term choreography has been often used in relation to my films. I would not call it that because faces cannot be choreographed. The space is being choreographed by the continuous action that forces this space to open and close like an accordion. The editing is internal and a sequence that might require ten shots in the conventional system of editing is now conveyed in one, which contains all ten because it can literally be cut in as many shots. I did this by not excluding the so-called dead time, the silences.

Contrary to the American model that demands multiple angles for every single scene, I believe that for each shot there is one angle and one angle only. This, for me, is a basic rule of the game. Something we have not discussed is the way I use the fixed shot. For example, the rape scene in my last film *(Landscape in the Mist)* is a fixed shot where the sound has more meaning than the image we see. In this fixed shot, the sound functions in a way that gives rhythm to the space, while simultaneously it creates a second level of meaning outside the film. It is like a painting that does not end inside the frame but continues outside of it. Likewise the power of suggestion is exercised dynamically in order to free the imagination of the audience, so they can create for themselves a picture inside the picture. The audience exists dynamically and not passively, when they add their imagination to that of the director. Of course you know very well that in Greek tragedy all the important events take place on stage and never behind the stage. For me, the tracking shot creates an accordion of space through the travelling of the camera. The space expands or shrinks depending on the proximity of the lens to the filmed objects; there is a continuous flow that brings incredible flexibility inside the shot, like the flow of running water.

For the filming of *The Travelling Players* the camera was always on a moving track even if it had to move ten centimeters in order to create a flow. The 360-degree shot is used to emphasize the meaning of the circle that already exists as a concept inside the film. In *Megalexandros,* it is obvious the circle is part of all forms, and it evolves from the circular stage of the ancient theater where all action was being performed. Look, today when someone begins to make cinema, cinema is his starting point. My generation began differently. My development was influenced by literature. I began by writing poems and short stories and only then did I move to film. Therefore I am influenced by a different space, where the act of writing is the dominant rule of the game. Consequently I sought the same in cinema.

Q: *Your Buffalo retrospective opens with* The Beekeeper, *and I would like to pose two questions about that film, both relating to icons or images. It is the first film in which you have used a major international "star." Marcello Mastroianni offers a very distinct icon, developed over many other works, to any film in which he acts. How did you understand that icon, and how did you used it and, at the same time, refashion it? The other question involves the relationship between the written script and the actual process of shooting. Every aspect of the mise-en-scène—Spyros's house, the hotels he stays in, his boyhood home, his destination itself, not to mention jukeboxes and soda pop stands—take on aspects of a beehive. Is that very complicated iconographic presence already designed at the outset or does it develop as the film is being shot, and how does this process take place?*

A: My intention was to use Mastroianni but to reverse the image he projects. I was looking for an actor who could carry the film on his shoulders. The role excluded any display of virtuosity and demanded a style of acting that is esoteric and silent, and this, I think, is the opposite of the image Mastroianni has been projecting. I was afraid that any other actor and mainly the ones I know here in Greece would have been crushed by the weight of this role. Mastroianni, on the contrary, carried the film not only because he is a good actor but also by using this weight as an image.

Sometimes my films are the exact mirror of the script; other times, the script is in the form of notes and then the filming process is very dependent on improvisation. In some cases, there is a dynamic that allows you to use improvisations, while in others you have the feeling that you have to follow exactly the written script. This depends entirely on the material you have to work with and does not depend at all on the circumstances surrounding the making of the film. The circumstances I have encountered until now vary from the very good to the very bad, but it did not prevent me from doing what I intended to do. For example, *Landscape in the Mist* is an exact copy of the script while *The Travelling Players* began from notes. *Voyage to Cythera* is very far from the original script and *The Beekeeper* very close to it.

I write the scripts and try them on the various people I have conversations with, like a game of Ping-Pong, where they act either as devil's advocates or as catalysts. This dialogue with other persons becomes essential to the writing of the script; it is a process of continuous inventions that occur only during the time I converse with them. The image from which I began the *Voyage to Cythera* was of the two old people on a raft in the middle of the sea. For *Landscape in the Mist* the first image was that of a city covered in fog and a hand that dissolves it.

Silence Is as Meaningful as Any Dialogue: *The Suspended Step of the Stork*

EDNA FAINARU / 1991

Q: *You have just finished a TV interview—it's almost as if we have stepped into your own film, whose leading character is a TV reporter. Though you don't seem to be too keen on television as a whole.*

A: To tell you the truth, I recently tried to watch *The Battleship Potemkin* on television but it was simply impossible. I suppose a Bergman film might have been more suitable. Strong emotions and an abundance of close-ups, these are the kind of ingredients that will survive the transition to the small screen. But when a film makes extensive use of silence, when it is contemplative and landscapes are as important in it as the spoken word, television will never do it full justice. I am not talking only about my own films; this is true also for large epic westerns. Take, for instance, a scene everybody is asking me about, the wedding sequence in *The Suspended Step of the Stork*. There isn't one line of dialog in it and its effectiveness depends entirely on the theater being absolutely quiet. The slightest noise, people moving in their chairs, any disturbance, and the entire scene is ruined. For you are expected to listen to the silence, which is as meaningful as any dialog. Now, how can you imagine perfect silence at home in front of the television set with kids crying and the phone ringing?

Q: *I was rather surprised to see you chose for your film the point of view of a television reporter. Isn't it a bit too easy an artifice for you?*

Interview at Cannes Film Festival, May 1991. Excerpts published in *Tel Aviv Magazine*, May 1992. © 1992 by Edna Fainaru. Reprinted by permission. Translated by Dan Fainaru.

A : The truth is that I chose his point of view because it allows me to do things I usually wouldn't do. Close-ups, for instance, are generally out of place in my films. But thanks to the subterfuge of the TV camera, I could introduce two long close-ups of Jeanne Moreau, the first when she announces her husband's death, the other when she claims the man produced by the TV crew for her is not the person she's looking for. I felt close-ups were essential in these scenes, but I did not want to break the flow of the camera movement in the middle in order to insert them. Instead I put the TV set showing the close-up inside the shot covered by the camera. There were additional reasons for having a TV reporter in the story. At one point he says that all he did in the past is shoot people, a self-critical approach to his own profession. For cinema, unlike television, is trying to go beyond that, to reach into the dark recesses lurking behind the surface of the story and the people in it.

Q : *Your last film* Landscape in the Mist, *was an intensely personal and intimate film. This time you seem to keep your distances, as if to safeguard your perspective on the proceedings.*
A : First of all, this is a different type of movie. More epic, larger scope, more characters. Not to mention that it is all evolving around a missing person, and mystery has to be preserved all through it. For this reason you can never get too close to this person. In these circumstances, a close-up would be immoral, an invasion of privacy, more so since the character refuses to unveil his identity. It is essential to keep this mystery intact in order to substantiate his later decisions and to keep him inside that gray area between fact and fiction.

Q : *With every new film you seem to be more concerned by the fate of displaced persons, emigrants, refugees. The father of the children in* Landscape in the Mist, *who by the way we never see, is one of these persons. In* The Suspended Step of the Stork *you focus on a group of refugees.*
A : Emigration and diaspora, refugees chased away from their own homeland, crossing borders and seeking shelter, these are among the most burning social issues of our time. Not to mention the bankruptcy of the old ideals or the absence of moral authority that could offer some ulterior motive or goal to these wanderings. The missing father is the moral authority in *Landscape in the Mist*. And he is missing. In this film, there is no moral authority what-

soever. This is not a matter of opinion; it is a fact. Cinema, today, prefers to ignore this open, festering wound and look elsewhere. For instance, at artists in crisis whom the world refuses to accept, etc. Making a film about an artist and his model, that's the French version of looking at the world. Strangely enough, it is the Americans who are now turning back to political and social issues, dealing with racism and facing reality.

Q: *Are you trying to imply that all of us, to a smaller or greater extent, are emigrants in our own lands?*
A: Yes, I suppose we are all migrating birds moving from one place to another. To tell you the truth, I often feel a stranger in my own country. Sometimes, I'd like to act just like Mastroianni in the film and announce that I am a political refugee in my homeland.

Q: *The refugees in your film live in caravans next to the river. Everything seems to be prepared for the next move, and yet everybody is stuck in one place.*
A: True. Each one of them would like to start a new life in a new place. Mastroianni expresses it quite clearly when he says: "We crossed another border, how many more will we have to cross before we reach home?" He refers, of course, to the real home, the one place where a person feels he really belongs to, heart and soul. For me, this phrase sums up the entire film. This is the kind of existentialism you will not find in my earlier films.

Q: *All through the film you mention the year 1999, as if there is something symbolic about it.*
A: It's a myth. Just like the abstract concept of Germany, the place the two children are trying to reach in *Landscape in the Mist*. This year, 1999, should be the beginning of a new era, when the whole world will share one dream together, instead of the many personal, puny, bloody dreams they have today. And it doesn't matter whether they are Serbs and Croats, Greeks and Turks, or other dreams of a similar kind which tear people apart instead of bringing them together. Several years ago I saw a Yugoslav film, a love story between a Serb man and a Muslim woman in Kossovo [Srdjan Karanovic's *Film with No Name*, D. F.]. I believe there is a similar Israeli film about an Israeli man and an Arab woman [Nissim Dayan's *A Very Narrow Bridge*, D. F.]. This is a plague the world has to get rid of. We're going back to the wars of

religion. It's like going back to the crusades at the end of the millenium, it's ridiculous.

Q: *Speaking of religion, a scandal accompanied the shooting of* The Suspended Step of the Stork *in Greece. Some rumors were mentioning religious desecration, but seeing the film, it's difficult to understand what they were talking about.*
A: It was the doing of one single person, the bishop of Florina, the town where the movie was shot. Now that I have had the time to reflect and consider the entire affair, I suspect he was worried that his own authority might suffer. Traditionally, every politician and public figure visiting that place has to come and present their respects. Nothing goes on there without his blessing and God help those who dare infringe his instructions. Let me give you an example. The person who organizes the modest film club in town is a young pharmacist, about thirty. When he declared that he supported my film, he was immediately blacklisted. The townsfolk were instructed not to enter his pharmacy and never buy anything from him; he was about to go bankrupt. True, it is not a very common occurrence in Greece, but sometimes it happens.

Q: *It is all the more difficult to understand the bishop's position considering the crucial scene in your film, the marriage with the bridge on one side of the river and the groom on the other side, with only the auspices of the church to bring them together. By the way, your scene reminded me of similar moments in real life. Druse families in the Golan Heights, some of them living now in Israel, others in Syria, meet on weekends at the border, to shout messages at each other across the borderline.*
A: There are more cases like this. After completing the film, I saw in the newspapers photos of Azeris who come to the border between Azerbaijan and Iran to meet their families. The border there is a river too, just a little bit smaller than the one in my film. I can also tell you that in the village where I shot the film, the inhabitants told me that once the border was drawn and established in 1949, the Albanians prohibited any contact across it. They did it, despite the fact that the borderline often crossed fields owned by the same family, who found themselves, all of a sudden, living in two different countries. They couldn't meet each other again until forty years later. What happened then was that from each side of the border you could see people coming with old photos in their hands, showing these photos around and

trying to identify the relatives some of them had never seen before. It's terrible. I am not sure this kind of tragedy is within the grasp of everybody. When the French looked at *The Travelling Players,* their admiration was purely intellectual. Elsewhere, the reactions were actually physical. Once, in Hiroshima, when I visited the museum, a stranger approached me, a Vietnamese. He said he had seen my film and it is just like the story of his own family. His reaction was not at all intellectual; for him *The Travelling Players* was the chronicle of his family. I think, for instance, the Italians feel closer to the film than the French, because they had gone through fascism, Mussolini, and German occupation. As for the British, they were pleased by the irony in the film, particularly when it was directed at their own people. All of which proves a film is accepted or rejected not only on its own merits, but also because it does or does not suit a certain emotional climate, which changes from place to place.

Q: *All your previous films had, as their point of departure, the Greek mythology. Are there any similar origins in* The Suspended Step of the Stork?
A: No, there is no reference to Greek mythology here.

Q: *It seems that this film, more than any of those you made previously, expresses your reserves towards politics and politicians.*
A: Absolutely. This film rejects every aspect of politics. When the character Mastroianni plays in the film says: "There are times when silence is imperative for us to listen to the music behind the raindrops," what he really means is that all the pretentious political theories are useless; they all dissimulate the real music of life.

Q: *How did you reach that conclusion? After all, your films always contained strong political statements. Now you accept the opinion of those who claim it's all useless?*
A: I do not accept it, but I have to face it. What can I do? For a very long time we used to dream that politics was not a profession; it was a creed, a faith, an ideal. But in recent years, I have become convinced politics is nothing more than just another profession, that's all.

Q: *There are a number of recurrent themes in your films, be it the strong roots of the people you describe with the land they live on, the landscape of Northern Greece, even the marriage ceremony which seems to come back in all the films.*

A: As for the last part of the question, maybe the reason is that I, myself, never got married. I have three daughters but never married. There may be some Freudian interpretation to all this—could it be I am trying to compensate for something missing in my life? In any case I concede this is a recurrent theme in my films. There are others. Like children or very young people. But I am not sure how important all this is. Some film critics will tell me there are eighty shots in my film. So what, I know how many shots I have in the film, but does it really have any meaning except for researchers and film analysts? Would the film be that different if there were eighty-three shots instead of eighty?

Q: *In any case, there is no need for researchers to notice this is your darkest film to date. Visually everything in it is dark gray. It seems this is the predominant color of your film.*
A: In this case, I must confess to an error. When we prepared the print that was to be screened in Cannes, we did not calculate correctly the intensity of the projector's light. We were under the impression the light is stronger, and for this reason we brought over a darker print. For the benefit of all those who will screen the film in future, it shouldn't be any darker than *Landscape in the Mist*. I would say the predominant color in it is gray with a tinge of green.

Q: *In this film you reached the northern border of Greece. What are you going to do next, cross the border and shoot abroad—something you never did before?*
A: Maybe. I was twice in New York, and I must say I was very much impressed by it despite my original attitude, a kind of skeptical rejection of everything it had to offer. I would definitely like to try making a film there—something about relations between different ethnic communities.

Q: *If you do it, it could be considered almost a natural extension of your career. In the past, everything in your film—the landscape, the characters, the stories—they were all profoundly Greek. In* The Suspended Step of the Stork *there is a change. You deal with uprooted people. Their national identity is dubious; the one thing left is personal identity. Maybe it is time the landscape around should not be as precisely defined as it was in the past?*
A: Look, in New York I met people who have lived all their lives there and couldn't possibly live anywhere else. And yet, they feel displaced, no roots,

no home of their own. For this reason, they try to create substitutes, like the Greek quarter, Little Italy, Chinatown, the Jewish quarter. Why do they all feel the need to surround themselves with borders?

Q: *Would it be fair to say that the one-time revolutionary, who once burned with the desire to change the world, is now disillusioned, has settled down, a home and a family of his own, and has no longer the urge to rebel against the world?*
A: Not quite. Let's not forget that already in *Megalexandros*, when I was still very much guided by the spirit of '68, I was describing a revolutionary who turns into a tyrant. I was not referring to one specific example but to the danger of corruption facing every person in power. I needed five years after I finished my first trilogy (*Days of 36, The Travelling Players, The Hunters*), to start a second one that I would call *The Silence of History*. *Voyage to Cythera* puts to sleep the last of the great ideals of history, communism. Once that was over, nothing was left but to look inside, into one's own self. To face the identity crisis we're all victims of, or the void surrounding those who dare speak no more because they don't have anything new to say, unless it is to speculate about the end of history. My films have become far more personal and intimate; there is a central figure in them, whose traits, character, and dreams I explore through the film. *The Beekeeper* went one step further in this direction, expressing at the time a personal and professional crisis I was going through at that moment. But let me tell you, not only do I not settle down, as you implied, my reputation may be growing, but I am more revolted and bitter than ever before. The family has not changed at all. Having children means thinking about the future. The first ending I wrote for *Landscape in the Mist* showed the children lost in the fog. But then, I couldn't resist the sadness in my daughter's eyes when she read the script. I talked this over with her mother, and she said the girl was right. It's the truth, I am not making this up. One has no right to invent a fairytale with monsters in the shape of cranes and stone grinders, and take away from the audience even the modest relief of an open end. My daughter kept asking me: "Where is the house, where is the father?" I couldn't give her a proper answer, but I tried to reply in my own way, by putting that tree at the end. Also, I believe I am fully aware of everything that happens in this world of ours, and my films show it. Of course, I could claim, just like Borges, that I make my films for my friends and to ease the passing of time. But when Borges talks about friends, they could be just a couple, a few hundreds, thousands, or maybe

millions. I can only say that the Vietnamese person in Hiroshima profoundly touched me, and it has provided me with much food for thought. By the way, the same thing happened to me twice again. Once in Montreal, a second time in Bulgaria, where I met a girl whose father was Greek, her mother Russian, and who had the feeling of being a stranger wherever she went. She claimed *Voyage to Cythera* is, in every detail, the story of her own father. And I could mention one more instance, an encounter I had in the north of Greece, while looking for suitable locations to shoot this film. The cameraman and the set designer had come along. We were in a miserable mood, worried that we might be lost, wandering around a deserted mountain village. These were the last days of summer. The peasants, mostly shepherds, were about to leave for the winter with their sheep; only one of them was supposed to stay there, to keep an eye on the place until next summer. Before they left, they gave a small party. By the time we got there most of them were already gone. Just a few remained, and when we walked in they looked at us as if we were ghosts. The set designer, tired and nervous, accused me of dragging him and the cameraman there for no purpose whatsoever. One of the shepherds heard the conversation and asked me if I was indeed Angelopoulos. When I said "Yes," he told me he had seen all my films and then addressed an old man sitting next to him and asked him whether he remembered seeing a film about a woman who kills her husband [he was referring to Angelopoulos's first film, *Reconstruction*, D. F.]. Since they were using a local slang, and since the film's narrative was hardly conventional, I wondered whether they had understood it at all. But both said they were very familiar with this kind of story, they had lived through similar episodes. These echoes, coming from such different corners of the world, are terribly important for an artist. I suppose, for some, it just satisfies their greed, selling more tickets. But for many of us, it is the living proof that our work is not in vain, that through it we can reach other human beings, across borders and oceans, who may be feeling and thinking just like we do.

National Culture and Individual Vision

ANDREW HORTON/1992

CINEASTE: *Your most recent film,* The Suspended Step of the Stork, *is very contemporary in its treatment of borders, refugees, and a changing world since the fall of communism in Eastern Europe and the former Soviet Union. What is your particular interest in "refugees"?*
THEO ANGELOPOULOS: Marcello Mastroianni, the main character, says in the film, "Being a refugee is an *internal* condition more than an external one." Later on he also says, "We've passed the borders but we're still here. How many frontiers do we have to pass to get home?"

CINEASTE: *Could you relate this to the current situation of Greece's northern neighbor, the former Yugoslavia?*
ANGELOPOULOS: It is impossible for us to understand why, at the end of the twentieth century, we are killing each other. Do professional politicians anywhere really care? Many nations, including Greece, are climbing over the bodies of murdered innocent people, most recently in Greece—I am referring to slaughtered Albanians who wish to leave home—in order to make some *political* advantage. I want a new politics in the world with vision. And this will not be a simple matter of balancing an economy and the military. It must be a new form of communication between people.

CINEASTE: *Some of your images and long takes are so unusual that it's hard to imagine scripting them. How much are you inspired on location? How much improvisation is involved?*

From *Cineaste*, vol. 19, no. 2/3, December 1992. © 1992 by CINEASTE. Reprinted by permission.

ANGELOPOULOS: My first film, *Reconstruction,* was almost one hundred percent based on the scenario. My second work, *Days of '36,* was also quite close to the script. But *The Travelling Players* included a *lot* of improvisation. In the scene, for instance, in which two different political groups begin to "fight" by singing opposing songs, a lot of what finally made it into the film came from the dynamics of the rehearsals. In another scene, when the group of actors walks along a road in the snow, singing, and winding in between each other, not a word appears in the script: it was simply a cut between two scenes. Yes, I am influenced by the location, the landscape, what is going on with the actors.

I like to have a screenplay as a base and then build on it, branch out. *Landscape in the Mist* is once again close to the script; but *Voyage to Cythera* was just the opposite. As one can see, it became a film about making a film, thus a "work in progress." The whole scene at the end, when the main character and his wife are set afloat on a barge, was improvised.

CINEASTE: *You are often referred to as a director who is as far away from any American style of shooting and narrative as a filmmaker can be. But you say you appreciate American cinema.*
ANGELOPOULOS: My first love in films as a boy were American genre films—Westerns, musicals, and gangster films. Melodramas a bit, too, but not so much. I particularly liked John Ford, Michael Curtiz, and Minnelli's musicals.

CINEASTE: *Would you say more about your interest in Hollywood's musicals?*
ANGELOPOULOS: If we go back to the singing "battle" scene in *The Travelling Players,* we see it is a musical! What I liked in the Hollywood musical was the freedom to be very stylized and to take off from daily life into something else. The American musical moved from a sense of reality to a theatrical one, like Gene Kelly in *Singin' in the Rain.* I have just returned from a retrospective of my films in Ireland, and the whole country, especially the people in the pubs, are completely musical! So I feel the musical form allows you to transform daily life into *something else.*

CINEASTE: *In* The Suspended Step of the Stork *you use the Beatles song, "Let It Be," with one of the characters singing it in English in a key scene. Why that particular song in 1991?*

ANGELOPOULOS: Because the Beatles are enjoying a revival with the young people in Greece and Europe at the moment and I wanted to convey such a feeling.

CINEASTE: *In Russia, critics and film fans often talk about the "spiritual" leaders in cinema with, of course, Andrei Tarkovsky leading the pack because of his deeply personal meditations on human nature and the lack of spirituality in a modern world. With your body of films, which question much of Greek and modern life, are you the spiritual leader of Greek cinema?*

ANGELOPOULOS: I am in a very strange position in Greece. I have fanatic enemies and fanatic followers. That's all I can say! Two generations of Greeks have grown up with my films now, and I meet many people who tell me or write me that my films have changed their lives.

CINEASTE: *In* Landscape in the Mist, *a young Greek girl is raped in the back of a truck by a truck driver, but we see nothing. We need not remark how many movies these days contain graphic rape scenes, whether justified or not. In contrast, you concentrate on a long, slow tracking shot towards the back of the truck afterwards, when the girl slowly sits up and examines her bloody hand. Would you comment on how you planned and shot that scene?*

ANGELOPOULOS: We shot that scene last even though it appears halfway through the film It was shot exactly as I wrote it, for I was careful to construct it so as not to disturb the girl, Tania Palaiologou. So, of course, I did not want to show the rape. Even so, she wasn't sure she could do the scene. That's why we waited until the end.

CINEASTE: *Many films from the Balkans, Eastern Europe, Russia, Greece, and other countries have rape scenes that are particularly cruel. They are viewed not from the point of view of the victim, but as an acceptable form of male behavior. In a rape scene such as the one we have discussed, you appear to undermine a macho mentality and show sympathy for women. There is a similar effect in* The Travelling Players.

ANGELOPOULOS: It is true I do not wish to support any macho perspective. In fact, I feel that any society that is strongly centered around the penis, that is, the phallus, is disturbing. Here in Greece and Italy, for instance, countries that have always been known as very male centered, things are definitely changing. Women have clearly gained new freedoms.

CINEASTE: *Do the men accept this?*
ANGELOPOULOS: Of course not! [*laughs*] Look at my first film, *Reconstruction*. It is told from the perspective of the woman, a wife who kills her husband. And there is the scene in *The Travelling Players* when the woman just laughs at the man who strips in front of her. I don't mean to say I am a feminist, for I'm against any orthodox ideology, but I do believe that we should encourage people—men and women, black, white, or yellow—to use their brains in relation to their bodies.

CINEASTE: *Many filmmakers have begun to say that, in an age of television, video, and computers, the time for highly individualistic director's films may be over. Some even say the time for cinema is past.*
ANGELOPOULOS: NO! The world needs cinema now more than ever. It may be the last important form of *resistance* to the deteriorating world in which we live. Many write to me—I am talking about everyone from simple people to important folk in politics, film, culture, business—and say that my last film, *The Suspended Step of the Stork*, was a film that *had* to be made because it catches so much of the tension today. You see, in dealing with borders, boundaries, the mixing of languages and cultures today, the refugees who are homeless and not wanted, I am trying to seek a new humanism, a new way.

CINEASTE: *But most people who will see your films today will see them on video or TV, not on the big screen. It's hard to imagine a director who will suffer more than you from the small screen because of your sense of composition of landscapes and locations in relation to characters.*
ANGELOPOULOS: Unfortunately you may be right. Personally I do not let people I know see my films on tape. I ask everyone to go to the cinema.

CINEASTE: *With your precise sense of composition, are you influenced by the Byzantine tradition of icon painting?*
ANGELOPOULOS: Of course, the influence is there. You cannot help but be influenced by a place and its culture when you grow up there, especially at a particular time, as I did, when the church was an important part of my cultural (not necessarily religious) life. *Megalexandros* is completely a Greek Orthodox or Byzantine work, because it is constructed on many elements of the Orthodox liturgy, combining music, ritual, and the *catharsis* through

blood. And, of course, the role of the icon in all of this. But such an Orthodox or Byzantine influence is not the only Greek influence. In *Megalexandros* I also make use of the tradition of Greek shadow puppet shows, *Karanghyosis*. In some scenes I copied the *Karanghyosis* shows exactly, including the way the Alexander the Great puppets are used in them.

CINEASTE: *Part of the icon tradition is the sense in which icons are linked together to form a "program" within a church, a visual series that is complete, united.*

ANGELOPOULOS: World cinema thinks of Eisenstein when we say "montage of attractions." Then there is Hollywood's sense of "parallel cutting" developed from Griffith. But what interests me is what I think of as montage *within the scene*. In my films, montage exists not through the cut, but through *movement*. I feel montage can be created through the continuous shot involving *time* and movement which involves *space*. In these shots of mine, time becomes space and space becomes time. Think how important the "pause" is in those spaces between action or music. They are very important in creating the total effect. My scenes are complete units, but the pauses between them are what really unite all as one. Perhaps *The Hunters* is the one film of mine closest to a musical. You can almost count the beats of the scenes like those of a song.

CINEASTE: *What would you say about the importance of humor and comedy? Is it a conscious part of your work?*

ANGELOPOULOS: I believe in humor, but in my films it comes out as ironic humor. For instance, there is the scene in *The Travelling Players* where the actors slowly close in on a lone chicken in the midst of a snowy landscape and all attack it together since they are starving. So many people attacking one chicken! It is funny, but it is dark humor. There is a lot of such humor, in fact, in *The Travelling Players*. And there is much irony in *Days of ;36*. It is present in *The Hunters*, but more hidden. In *The Suspended Step of the Stork*, the humor and playfulness of the TV crew among themselves only serve to make the film more despondent since it is clear that, no matter how tragic events are around them, they just want to have a good time.

CINEASTE: *You have said previously that the Greece you show—the countryside, the North, the abandoned villages, filmed at dawn or dusk and often in winter—is an effort to create an interior Greece. Would you say more?*

ANGELOPOULOS: Athens and life in this city, where forty percent of the Greek population lives, is a *deformed* image of Greek life. It is an interesting image, but not a true one. You see, it is very difficult to break through the sense of daily life in Athens and see what is behind it. If you see only Athens, you have a false view of Greece. That is why I work in that Other Greece. I want to see if I can break open this Athenian reality. On the other hand, it would certainly be worthwhile to do for Athens what Joyce did for Dublin in *Ulysses*. But that's not my project. I suppose I don't try that because it is my own childhood and I do not want to destroy it!

CINEASTE: *If we think of two kinds of films, those that work towards a sense of shared community, such as John Ford's films, or, on the other hand, those that highlight the alienation of the protagonist, as in Chaplin walking alone down the road, where do you fall?*
ANGELOPOULOS: Closer to John Ford, of course. The ending of *The Suspended Step of the Stork*, when we see so many men climbing telephone poles to connect wires, is clearly about communication, getting people in touch with each other.

CINEASTE: *Finally, your films are voyages, journeys. Would you comment on this major theme/structure in your work?*
ANGELOPOULOS: *Landscape in the Mist*, for instance, is not just about two children looking for their father. It is a journey which is the initiation into *life*. On the road they learn everything—love and death, lies and truth, beauty and destruction. The journey is simply a way to focus on what life gives us all. In *Voyage to Cythera* the voyage is really a reworking of the myth of the Return of Odysseus according to a myth which preceded Homer. Similar to Dante's version, there is a pre-Homeric version that Odysseus set sail again after reaching Ithaca (of course, Nikos Kazantzakis also chose this myth to represent in his *The Odyssey: A Modern Sequel*). So the film becomes more a leaving than a homecoming. You see, I have a soft spot for the ancient writings. There really is nothing new. We are all just revising and reconsidering ideas that the ancients first treated!

Homer's Where the Heart Is: *Ulysses' Gaze*

GEOFF ANDREW/1996

ASK EVEN THE BUFFIEST of your friends to name a Greek movie and, like as not, after some thought they'll come up with *Zorba the Greek* or, at a pinch, *Never on Sunday*. Mercifully, however, Greek cinema isn't all hoary old tosh about life-affirming beach-dances, bouzoukis, and Melina Mercouri: however minor a movie industry it may have, the land that gave us Homer, tragedy, and the first philosophers and historians has also spawned Theo Angelopoulos, one of the most distinctive and distinguished filmmakers working in the world today.

Theo who? Exactly. Because his output has been little seen other than at festivals or, just occasionally, on television, the sixty-year-old writer-director hasn't received anything like the recognition he deserves. Prejudices about Greek movies haven't helped; nor, probably, have his concerns—the spiritual, moral, and political condition of modern Greece and Europe, filtered in part through allusions to ancient myth—or his style, whereby naturalism, Brechtian theatricality, and wordless reverie are seamlessly integrated by means of long, fluid takes whose complexity, elegance, and audacity outdo even the celebrated travelling shot that opened Welles's *Touch of Evil*.

Yet the rewards to be had from Angelopoulos's stately odysseys—1975's *The Travelling Players,* probably his best known film here, lasted almost four hours though it consisted of only 131 shots—are considerable. Greece, here, is not some sunny, clichéd idyll but a grey, wintry scattering of small, characterless towns, desolate truck-stops, dingy hotel rooms, and empty squares;

From *London TimeOut,* Feb. 14–21, 1996. © 1996 by TimeOut. Reprinted by permission.

the past, both distant and recent, hangs heavy over Angelopoulos's heroes—whether aging, disillusioned men (as in *Voyage to Cythera* and *The Beekeeper*) or runaway, fatherless children (*Landscape in the Mist*)—as they journey in search of . . . well, some sense of purpose or future. Time is literally of the essence in these movies: a single sequence-shot will often take in not only different places, perspectives, and groups of people, but different eras (even, in the case of *Megalexandros,* millennia apart). The result is at the very least poetic and thought-provoking; usually, it's mesmerizingly beautiful, with any bleakness in tone more than counterbalanced by the exhilarating perfection of the meticulous direction. All you need is a little patience: as Harvey Keitel told Angelopoulos, "In the time you take for one shot, Tarantino makes a whole film!"

Which brings us to *Ulysses' Gaze,* in which a Greek filmmaker (Keitel) returns for a retrospective of his work in the town of his birth after thirty-five years in America. The real reason for his homecoming, however, is personal: obsessed with tracking down three legendary, long-lost reels of film by the Manakia Brothers—the first footage ever shot in the Balkans—he embarks on a trip that takes him through Albania, Macedonia, Bulgaria, and Romania, to Belgrade and, finally, Sarajevo. As with all Angelopoulos's best work, the film transcends the specificity of its setting to treat more universal concerns: the problematic nature of national borders (both geographical and psychological), the futility of war, film's relationship to history and politics, the unending quest for love, innocence, and a sense of personal identity. At once epic and deeply personal, it's the filmmaker's most accessible work to date.

"In recent years," says the genial Angelopoulos, "I've been preoccupied with ideas about exile and the journey, both exterior and interior—with the possibility of dreaming in this end-of-the-century world where there's an absence of dreams. Now, it seems, we just live from day to day, and it's hard really to believe in something. For me, 'home' is not your house, but a place where you feel in harmony—which in my case is in a car passing through a landscape—and what counts is not arriving but the journey itself. So in this film, the hero's homecoming is also a departure, the beginning of a new journey.

"I wanted to make a film somehow related to *The Odyssey,* and when I visited my co-writer, Tonino Guerra, who I'd already worked with on four films, we talked over what sort of journey it might be. Then we began to discuss the ethnic conflict in the Balkans, and as we spoke, a young woman arrived, sent by the daughter of the Italian sculptor Giacomo Manzù, with a present for Tonino. And there was a letter from Manzu's daughter saying how he used to have an *idée fixe* about the gaze of Ulysses, who in his travels had seen the entire human adventure. And that's how we came to the title of our film."

While Angelopoulos denies the film is autobiographical in terms of the events it depicts (Keitel is called "A" in the screenplay and pressbook" because we had to call him something"), he does admit that it's *"spiritually* autobiographical: it's about my ideas, the questions I ask about the Balkans, the cinema, the human condition. I do know what civil war is—my father, for example, was condemned to death during the Greek Civil War, and though he wasn't executed, my family ended up divided against each other—but I'm no political analyst. I can't say this side is good, this is bad; I simply speak about people suffering the consequences of the madness of war, whichever side they're on.

"The problems in the Balkans are especially complex because they go back such a long way, to when various Slavic tribes came under the Ottoman Empire in the fourteenth century. There were no borders in the Empire, but there were wars, even though it wasn't *ethnic* conflict: it was about conquering land, having enough to eat. Then, with parts of the region passing from the Islamic Turks to the Austro-Hungarian Empire, which was Catholic, and with the French Revolution's ideas of the nation state, all these peoples—Greeks, Serbs, Bulgars, and so on-were mixed up together, and started having religious and ethnic conflicts. So it's a very old story. And of course it's Sarajevo where World War I began; so while many places have seen as much or more destruction than Sarajevo, it's become a symbolic, almost mythic place."

Like his hero, Angelopoulos is also intrigued by the Manaki Brothers who, in the early 1900s, travelled the Balkans filming whatever they saw; while Balkan states stressed their national and ideological differences, the Brothers' documentary-style footage reflected cultural similarities. Hence "A" 's hope that in rediscovering the lost Manaki footage, he'll be able to restore an "innocence" to his own cinematic gaze.

"I'm always fascinated by what comes first: the first films, or one's first experience of film. Fellini once said that when he first put his eye to the camera, he found that what had seemed certain, familiar, now seemed strange; and that's true. The earliest image I recall from my filmmaking life was when I began my first feature, *Reconstruction,* in an old, remote mountain village where a man just back from working as a *gastarbeiter* in Germany had, like Agamemnon, been murdered by his wife and her lover. I arrived there: it was grey, raining slightly; some old women in black disappeared into the vineyards; I heard someone singing a love song in a distant café. And that image, that sound, that rain," he laughs, "perhaps that single moment has influenced all the films I've made since!

"As for my long takes—well, there are filmmakers with a very different style whose work I very much enjoy. And while there's a stylistic difference between, say, Hemingway and Faulkner, you wouldn't have asked either of them, 'Why do you write that way?' It's just a kind of interior development, interior rhythm. For me, my style is a way of trying to assimilate space and time, so that space *becomes* the passing of time. For example, one sequence in this film, set in one room, is not at all in real time: five years—five years in the history of one family, of Romania, and of Europe from the concentration camps to Stalinism—pass during a short waltz. Also, in cinema there's a fear of 'dead time': shots are cut in case there's not enough action. I suppose long sequence shots do go against the grain when cinema is generally moving towards greater efficacy, but there've been other filmmakers, too, who've moved in another direction: Mizoguchi, Ozu, Murnau, Antonioni—mainly Europeans and Asians. But even in some John Ford films you have quite lengthy shots; the American cinema has changed a lot."

Not that Angelopoulos is *against* Hollywood as such; indeed, he was keen from the start to cast Keitel as his lead, partly because "he possesses something very sensitive," partly because (by way, perhaps, of consciously reversing the usual Hollywood-Europe interchange) he was stimulated by "the challenge of using an American actor, but in my own way." Nevertheless, his films are emphatically at odds, stylistically and thematically, with the modern Hollywood norm. Given his hero's nostalgic quest for a more "innocent" gaze, does he himself feel, now that it's a hundred years old, that there's hope for a purer, more serious cinema? "There *is* a crisis in Europe, in terms of audiences, in that American films occupy upwards of 80 percent of the screens in certain countries. It's like an empire, and so we're getting an American education in many respects. I'm not against that so much, but I am against monopolies. It's our differences that are interesting, and if all the world becomes the same, it'll be very, very boring."

The Human Experience in One Gaze: *Ulysses' Gaze*

DAN FAINARU/1996

Q: *Let's start with an easy question. What are the origins of the script?*
A: I went, as usual before I start a new script, to visit Tonino Guerra in the North Italian village where he lives and told him this time I would like to do an Odyssey. Marvelous idea, he said, but how are you going to do it? First we thought of doing the Odyssey on the stock exchange. Then he went out and bought a copy of the *Odyssey* in Italian and he would read to me passages from it. When he reached the point when Ulysses comes home and Penelope does not recognize him, there was a knock at the door. A girl came in and said she was sent from the Manzù foundation (named after sculptor Giacomo Manzù) and was carrying a letter and a present for me. The present was a sculpture of Ulysses' head, and the letter was from Manzù's daughter. In it, she said that since I am Greek, she felt I should have this present and added that her father's last wish was to find a way of sculpting Ulysses' gaze because he believed this gaze contained the whole human experience. Here we were discussing the *Odyssey* and suddenly this surprise. Tonino thought that was a sign from heaven and decided we should pursue in this direction.

Q: *Your film can be approached on several levels: the history of the Balkans in the twentieth century; the history of cinema from its early beginnings up until today; the portrait of a film director in crisis; his yearning for the love of an ideal woman; and finally, this is also a political film, touching upon the recent events in Bosnia.*

From *All Cinema*, a Kol Israel radio show, broadcast October 1996. © 1996 by Dan Fainaru.

A: As I said, my point of departure was the Odyssey. I am referring to the myth, not to Homer's text. It is the same myth I used before in *Voyage to Cythera*. According to the myth, Ulysses comes back to Ithaca but does not stay there. After a while he leaves again on another journey. The film itself is the personal journey of a man, a filmmaker we know as "A," seeking a way out of a crisis that is not only his own, but that of an entire generation. He questions himself whether can he still see clearly the things that are going on around him, can he still create, is there anything more for him to discover, and any new things for him to invent? To a great extent, his crisis is my own too. The film is also a journey through the Balkan and European history of the twentieth century, in search of the three lost reels of the original Manaki films, a search that takes us across the history of cinema, which, as it happens, is also that of our century. The two Manaki brothers are not fictional characters; they were two brothers just like Auguste and Louis Lumiére, the first to make films in the Balkans. This search is not only for the reels themselves but also for what they represent, discovering the innocence and purity of the first shot taken by a camera, the kind of excitement which we seem to have lost forever. As for the love story, the object of his affection seems to change four times, but it is always the same face, one actress playing four roles. The face, the ideal woman that every adolescent dreams of as his romantic ideal.

Q: *Since you mentioned Greek mythology, it seems to be the source of most of your films, but somehow, the Greek light appears to have inspired you less.*
A: It's probably true. There is only one film I made, *The Days of '36,* that used the full impact of the Mediterranean sun, because the light you refer to is not typical to Greece only but to all the Mediterranean countries. That, and a documentary on Athens I shot in 1983. These are the only films I shot in the sun. All the others take place in winter, are immersed in fog, rain, snow, gray skies. I suppose this corresponds to a personal inclination of mine. The landscapes in my film are not necessarily the image of Greece—they are images of Greece, as I see it.

Q: *When you refer to the innocence and original purity of the first look, what do you mean?*
A: I am not talking about the innocence of children or that of an old peasant woman. The innocence I am concerned with is the innocence preceding

the discovery. Are we still sufficiently innocent and available emotionally to face a miracle and recognize it as such?

Q: *Do you have the feeling that after a hundred years of cinema, we have lost that quality?*
A: I am afraid we are submerged under far too many images. We are bombarded by TV images attacking us from every direction to such an extent that we have no longer the sensibility to discover the real gems that might come our way.

Q: *You're not very optimistic about the future of cinema either. In this film there are at least two cinemas in ruins.*
A: There is only one, I think . . .

Q: *There is another one, earlier on, at Iannina.*
A: Yes, you are right, that was the original Manaki cinema destroyed in 1938 by a fire while they were showing a Chaplin film. The film stock, at the time, as you know, was nitrate-based, easily inflammable. Yes, there are two cinemas in ruins, and now that I think of it, it's a recurring theme in several of my films. For example, in *The Beekeeper*. Let's face it, these days more cinemas than ever are converted into supermarkets. In our villages, many cinemas were turned into stables. It's so sad to see it all happening. We know that European cinema is not doing very well lately; less tickets are sold. The theatres today are no longer that privileged place of encounter between the creative artist and his audience. There is a small elitist minority still looking for that encounter, but the vast majority is favoring the American movies, which, as far as I am concerned, are not films but just images printed on celluloid.

Q: *The Florina episode at the beginning of this film is an authentic incident. The bishop residing there used all his influence to prevent the screening of* The Suspended Step of the Stork *because he felt he had been slighted when the film was shot. The screening took place in an improvised theatre and most of the audience were left outside, but stayed just to listen to the soundtrack—despite the church bells that were ringing to disturb them. You attended this screening, as you do in many towns all over Greece to help the distribution of your films. Is this personal involvement of the filmmaker in what is basically a commercial aspect necessary in the present state of cinema?*

A: First of all, we have to face the problems and recognize them for what they really are. For several years I have been participating in seminars, conferences, and encounters to discuss the crisis of modern cinema. It's become a fashionable event. There is always someone like Jacques Lang (French Culture Minister at the time) and many leading European directors. Everybody agrees the cinema is in crisis and then we go back to whatever we did before. We have to accept the fact that the state of cinema today, outside the U.S., reflects also the state of the world we live in. It is on this front that we have to fight in order to maintain our respective cultures, languages, our national traditions and characteristics. If Europe wants to preserve its specific image and qualities, it is essential to make a concentrated effort and help the cinema, provide it with the space and means it needs in order to express itself freely. As for the filmmakers, they should do their best to help their films attract as much attention as possible. I do it, I meet audiences all over the world and, of course, in every corner of Greece and discuss my films with them. But I realize that not every filmmaker can do it.

Q: *You mentioned that* Ulysses' Gaze *is, among other things, a love story. But is it really about love or the impossibility of loving? At one point, your protagonist says, "I am crying because I cannot love you."*

A: That phrase is taken from Homer's *Odyssey*. Ulysses remained seven years on Calypso's island, but he would often go down to the sea and cry. For he could not love Calypso; he was always thinking of Penelope. He wanted to love her, but couldn't. As a matter of fact, at the end of my film, the hero meets once again his first love. It's a film about firsts—first love, first look, the initial emotions that will always be the most important in one's life.

Q: *Twice in the film you mention a Bulgarian city, Plovdiv, but call it by its Greek name, Philipopoulis. Why?*

A: Yes, it's true. Philip the Second, who was the King of Macedonia and the father of Alexander the Great, founded the city, and there are many Greeks who still live there. The Bulgarians have changed its name, but I understand they consider now the possibility of reverting once again to the ancient, original name. At the time the episode in the film took place, people usually referred to it as Philipopoulis, whatever the official name. And indeed, at the border, when "A" uses the Greek name, the customs officer corrects him and says, "Plovdiv."

Q: *By doing it this way, was it your intention to say that the various Balkan populations have blended into each other to such an extent that they are by now one people?*
A: During the uprising against the Turkish occupation, there were those who were dreaming of unification of the Balkans, with the exception of Turkey, of course. At the time, the Turks were ruling all the Balkan nations with an iron fist. Personally, I could consider, in an ideal future, the inclusion of Turkey as well in this unified nation of the Balkans.

Q: *How can you hope to make the rest of the world understand the Balkan situation?*
A: I have to say that we learned many things while shooting this film, which took much longer and covered a lot more territory than you might think by just looking at the film. I believe that anyone who pretends to have something to say about the Balkans should, first of all, go on a long, extensive trip through this area, get to know the people and their particularities, and there are many of them. There is a poem saying "the more you know, the more you love, the more you love, the more you know." I do not pretend to analyze the situation; I am just bringing forward my own emotions and those of the characters in the film. And when the film speaks about the original innocence of the first look, it does not refer to cinema only. It is about the necessity in general to see the world once again without any preconceived ideas, as if for the first time. You know, this tendency of seeing old films, which is spreading nowadays, is in a way the expression of the nostalgia for the innocence of the films and of the spectators of the early days.

Q: *The procession of Lenin's statue on the Danube seems to me a twofold reference to religion, now such a big issue in the part of the world. The communist religion falling apart, on the one hand, and the peasants crossing themselves as the barge with the statue on it proceeds majestically down the river, on the other hand. It's as if these peasants are desperately in need of a religion, never mind which kind.*
A: The confusion which has taken the place once occupied by religion, deprives these people of the much needed "magic assistance," as Erich Fromm used to call it. This episode originated in a real scene I witnessed while they

were dismantling this huge statue to put it on a ship. A small boat with a couple on it was crossing the harbor of Constanza, the Romanian port on the Black Sea. When the man noticed the enormous effigy of Lenin, he stood up and looked at it, dumbfounded. The woman put her hand over his eyes and crossed herself. However, let's not forget, in a manner of speaking this is also a funeral, and in such circumstances it is customary for people to make the sign of the cross.

Q: *In your earlier films, you were frequently moving from present to the past, often in the frame of one shot. Then you gradually adopted a linear type of narrative; now you once again use flashbacks, whether of the hero's past or the way he imagines somebody else's past. Is this a change of approach?*
A: The film deals with the history of this century; therefore the use of flashbacks is mandatory here. My feeling, in any case, is that the past is an integral part of the present. The past is not forgotten, it affects everything we do in the present. Every moment of our lives consists of the past and the present, the real and the imaginary, all of them blending together into one.

Q: *At the end, we see your hero watching the Manaki films, but we never see them.*
A: There are several ways of looking at this. I did shoot the scenes he sees, but finally we decided not to show them because it was too concrete. For me, the purpose of his search is the discovery of himself, and that is what the films should show. On the other hand, since we deal with characters that really existed, the Manaki brothers, pretending to show their films and showing something else instead would be an unnecessary falsification. Basically, by developing the film, "A" has reached his goal, that's the end of his search. It doesn't matter what is on the film; maybe it's just rushes that were never supposed to be shown. The journey leading to their discovery in Sarajevo today, this is the important thing.

Q: *How did you work with Keitel on this film? He comes from a completely different discipline of acting, speaks a different language, weren't there any conflicts between you?*
A: Sure enough, Harvey Keitel, with his Actors Studio training, needed lots of time to prepare. Mastroianni used to say, "I am a kid, tell me a story, tell me what to do and I'll do it." He couldn't care less about the Method. Keitel

was the Method personified. For instance, he constantly tried to delay the shooting of the final scene in *Ulysses' Gaze,* taking place in the ruins of the destroyed Cinematheque. He was terrified by the notion that it is the end. But we reached the point when there was nothing else to shoot, and we had to do it. We set up the scene, lighted it, and then Harvey said, "Theo, please give me a minute, I need to listen to a certain Sinatra song." We were in a small town near Athens. No way we could find there the record he asked for. A car was dispatched to bring it over. He put the record on, went into his corner, and then I heard terrible sighs; he was crying like a child and calling his mother. Maybe the song reminded him of his mother. We waited until he came out and announced he was ready. We took the shot but because he had cried so much before, he was completely empty. I grasped the problem and told him: "We followed your method, now we shall try mine." I sent everyone away from the set without exception. Keitel was accompanied by a personal secretary, a gym instructor, a dialog coach, a shrink, a whole team. His secretary came to me and asked: "Do you mean that Harvey, too, should leave the set?" I said, "Yes." Harvey didn't say a word and went away. When I was left alone, I started playing the film's music at full volume. Outside, they were all listening to it. When the music finished, I asked them all to come back. Keitel was furious. He came to me, screamed at me, "Fuck you, who do you think you are, God? You have no respect for others . . ." and so on. I felt he wanted to hit me. He came close to me, went on talking in the same fashion, but I didn't budge. After a while, he calmed down. I asked: "Are you ready?" He practically fell apart, recollected himself for a moment, and then we shot the scene. Once the shot was completed, Erland Josephson came over for his own scene. Amused, I told him what happened and then I noticed that Josephson, who was laughing with me, suddenly became uneasy. He had noticed Keitel approaching behind me and listening. For a moment I feared the eruption of a second dispute but nothing happened. All he said was "You are great, man."

Q: *One couldn't call you an optimist. There is a phrase in the film, spoken by Ivo Levi, the head of the Sarajevo archives: "If you undertook such a journey just to find a piece of film, you must be either full of hope or in a state of utter despair." Looking at this film, I wonder whether this grim image of the end of the century should be taken as an expression of utter despair or is there some hope left after all?*

A: I hope this is neither optimistic nor pessimistic but a faithful image of our times. Optimists usually turn their backs on reality; they invent false reasons for believing things have to improve. On the other hand, the only acceptable conclusion for pessimists is to stop and commit suicide. At the very end of my film, my characters imply that "the journey goes on." It means the search for a home will continue ["how many borders do we have to cross before we reach home" asks the voice off early in the film, using a phrase already featured in the previous Angelopoulos film, *The Suspended Step of the Stork*], home being that privileged place where we can be finally at peace with ourselves and with the rest of the world. The search is not over, the film is not over. In the words of Lars Gustafsson, probably the best contemporary Swedish novelist, "we never capitulate, we have to go on."

Q: *How do you explain your fascination for politics and journeys, and was this film a journey indeed? Did you cross the Balkans to shoot it? For example, was the Sarajevo scene shot there?*

A: My interest in politics and the Balkans is very easy to explain. Look at the history of this century and you will notice that its first momentous event took place in Sarajevo, and now, as we approach the end of the century, we are again in Sarajevo. This proves to what extent we all failed. Living in the Balkans, I am naturally much closer to the events, and much more concerned than the rest of Europe. I wanted to shoot in Sarajevo, but couldn't. Everything was lined up for us to go there. We were all ready to go, waiting for our plane in Ancona, when the plane that left before us was turned back because the bombing had started again. But we did our best to show on screen the concept of Sarajevo, of the war going on there, of a city under siege. And finally, I believe the concept of Sarajevo is more important in this case than shooting the scene itself there. Often you are in the right location, but the spirit of that location is lacking. We shot in two other towns destroyed by this war, at Mostar and Vukovar, both victims of the same tragedy.

The Time That Flows By: *Eternity and a Day*

GIDEON BACHMANN/1997

BRAKES SQUEAL. CARS STOP short at a red light in the crazy town traffic of the gray city of Thessaloniki, in northern Greece, once a historical site, now an industrial center.

From the four corners, groups of boys storm the dusty windshields of the stopped vehicles, vying with each other to polish these with a dirty rag. Some hold a luxury tool: a rubber squeegee. Noisy competition erupts among the four- to ten-year-olds.

A police car rushes up, doors fly open, a group of policemen spurt to catch the tiny offenders. Only one manages to escape: a passing motorist opens his car door for him, apparently without motive, a gesture, a human touch. The motorist is Bruno Ganz, out looking for the sense of his life on this day, which may be his last. That evening he is expected to enter hospital. It is uncertain whether he will ever leave it.

G.B.: *We meet at least once a year, but only every ten years we record a conversation. By now, that makes twenty years of changing moods, of developing ideas. How do you feel about the insoluble problems of our modern everyday? Twenty years ago you told me that if one couldn't make films, one could at least plant tomatoes, raise bees, harvest honey. Ten years ago you seemed more pessimistic than I saw you today, working on your set. Would you be willing to say something about how you, as a person and a filmmaker, have evolved in these twenty years?*

From *Film Comment*, July–August 1998. © 1997 by Gideon Bachmann. Reprinted by permission.

T.A.: As you know, the best time to talk about serious things is when you have finished a film, and not necessarily in the middle of a shoot, when you are still trying, yourself, to dress your own thoughts in a form which is still in the process of taking shape. But I'll try.

Surely you are not one of those directors who approach a new film with insecurity?
On the contrary: I belong with those who are never sure, not even when a film is finished. I am always, without stopping, searching, searching.

I suppose that means that filmmaking, for you, represents a form of search.
That's always been like that. I think I was the most sure of myself on the films that have most disappointed me in the end. I think the more sure you are in the beginning, the more likely you are to betray yourself, to flounder.

What then would give you security? Or gives you security?
I need to see the eyes of the others. Only in the regard of the viewer do I recognize what I have made. Without that regard, that look in their eyes, I don't know if I've done well, if I have expressed that which I had in my mind's eye.
    Mind you, I am content when in the moment of shooting it all seems to go the way I have imagined it. I see that the shot was okay. But when I see the rushes I say damn! Something is missing, there is some sort of inner lack. Something that lacks in me and something that lacks in the script. Why didn't he jump? After all, I had hoped that he would jump if I brought the boat close enough to the rock. But Bruno didn't jump. Mind you, I hadn't told him to jump, I had only quietly hoped he would.
    It's always hard for me to value properly that which actually goes on in the player's heart, or even to judge what goes on, in detail, at any moment, in the whole constellation of the production. I cannot judge early enough what the real substance is or will be, which provides clean air. . . .

How then can you even finish a film?
I can't. You will have noticed, if you look carefully, that my films never really end. To me they are all "works in progress." Like building sites. Do you know how often I write a script for the same film? Take this one: we are shooting the sixteenth version of the script! And I am still writing, while I'm shooting. I change, add, subtract, without cease.

Is that because things, during the shooting, slowly come to life, develop a personality of their own? Is it a magical process?
You say that so easily: *magical*. What does that mean, *magical*? How can you explain that in the night, *magical*? How can you translate that? In the doing, what sort of an image do you choose for the *magical*?

But that's the most important question there is! "Choosing the image" ... making words into pictures—isn't that what filmmaking is all about?
It's a painful process. There are losses, but you could win. There is such a thing as the right pictures, scenes that come alive by being expressed in the right pictures, but there are also scenes that lose something when materialized into images. You cannot "write" pictures like literature. Fellini used to say that when he had trouble in the transformation process, he would sit down and *write* the scene as if it were a literary work. It would then be very easy, when you *read* it. But that isn't cinema. For the cinema I am obliged to find the right formula, the right cinematographic formula. And that, of course, if the most difficult.

How do you write your cinema, then? With those very long takes?
I write very short sentences. Everybody knows I shoot long scenes, but only my closest collaborators know that I write these short sentences, almost like Hemingway.

Do you describe scenes or do you only write dialogue?
I write in prose, like a short novel. I do not do technical scripts. In fact, you could publish my scripts as literature. That's what I do now. Previously, I didn't "write" at all, in that sense. For my film *The Travelling Players* (*O Thiassos*, '75), there was no script. I had some notes that contained the essentials. The action and the historical events. But until the last moment I never knew, for example, how to get from one period to the next. There are a lot of things in that film that we worked out during the shooting, that happened *"pendant."*

In the shooting, not in the cutting?
No, while shooting. Or a day before a scene was shot. Or two hours before. Revelation! The solution!

Does every scene represent a specific problem?
There is always a key, a key that opens the scene. And you have to find it. Sometimes you never find it. Among my notes for *Travelling Players*, there was an empty, white sheet of paper. All it said was "1939–1952." I simply didn't know how to show the passage of that period in an image. Finally I found the solution a day before shooting it.

Do you still feel, nevertheless, that writing is simpler?
Writing is simpler. First of all, you are alone. You can sneak in an adjective, or take one out. But in the shooting, every element that you remove or that you add requires heavy weighing and decisions. Apart from that there are now the faces, the players, the actors, the persons. The situation, the conditions, the feeling of that particular morning. As you saw this morning, because of that one scene of Bruno and the car, the whole town was in an uproar, because they had to close a main artery to traffic, anger, delays. . . . Apart from that, every moment of time has its mood, its particular feeling. A bad mood, for example, which doesn't fit your scene and doesn't adjust.

And of course the fact that the lovely loneliness of writing is gone?
Yes, you are exposed to all these people; you can't make cinema alone. But of course that also brings you into contact with the qualities of these others, and with their imperfections. What does that really mean, "collaborators"? It's a word that can mean different things from moment to moment.

So there you are with all the usual compromises of filming.
Yes, you're not alone anymore. A lot of things were possible when you were writing, which must now, immediately and without help, be decided. That's why I now love the writing—you can imagine everything, can invent anything, create a world all of your own.

There are filmmakers who have always refused to consider film an artform because it cannot be controlled by an individual. Today, with digital equipment, these filmmakers feel that film might "again" become an artform, because a single person can—they think—do it all. When you cannot do everything yourself, you're forced, always, to enter into some form of compromise, so that your result is almost mathematically less successful than your intent. Do you believe in the new methods? Do

you believe that through them real, individual art may "again" become possible? Or maybe you feel it never ceased being possible?
Truffaut used to say that we are more intelligent than that which we produce. He also said—being conscious of the inevitable compromises—that it's like winning in a lottery when you succeed in creating everything the way you had imagined it. But the opposition of the conditions pursues you all your life. In fact, in the course of time you make some sort of peace with the opposing conditions, with the inevitable obstacles. You accept your films more readily. The time of pain is the time of the making. And immediately thereafter, when you present the film. At a festival, for example, or in front of a "normal" public.

Is that the moment, when the film, for you, is finished?
No. What finishes there is your relationship with the others. Your own relationship to the film doesn't end there. If sometime, in a quiet moment, you look at your film alone, that's when you know whether you can enter into peace with it, whether you accept it the way you made it.

Are you ever happy with a film you have made? Do you ever make peace with it?
As you know, I don't often look at my films. And when I do, of course, I immediately see the things I do *not* like, which I could have done differently. But there are films that I wasn't happy with at first which have slowly developed a life of their own, and which I now like better. For example, *Landscape in the Mist* (*Topio Stin Omichli*, '88): Today I find that to be one of the most touching films that I have made—in fact, I love that film.

And you've not made that film with your head alone, or you would have known earlier. Maybe the mind is a form of limitation. . . .
You know, everything is a limitation. As long as we talk about the things that help the artist or hinder him, and about how conscious a matter creation actually is.

Or how conscious is the choice of theme?
You mean because I've made three films in a row about borders, films in which borders are somehow the central theme?

I mean in the sense that choosing a theme, too, is a form of limitation. But unlike some limitations, it is one you impose upon yourself.

Borders for me are not geographical concepts, and I don't mean that there are borders in the sense of artistic limits, either. . . . Borders are simply divisions, between here and there, between then and now. In this film it is a question of a division between life and death. It's a demarcation line: a dying man, his last day. How do you pass your last day? What can still happen to us? What will we do with the hours that remain? Do you think back on the life you've lived? Or do you allow yourself to drift, expose yourself to all coincidences, follow someone, open a window, meet a new person, open yourself to anything that comes, to the unexpected coming-together of the unconnected, which then turns out to connect, after all?

In this case, is it the meeting with this young Albanese windshield cleaner? This robbed and sold child, for which you suddenly take responsibility, without knowing why, and whether you have the right to take it?
Yes, what can happen in such a meeting? What can grow out of it? Maybe everything? Maybe nothing. Now, at my age, I find it necessary to begin to devote some thought to death. In order to rediscover life. In order to see life in a new light, conscious of the fact that you have made peace with the idea of dying.

Is there a dialectic in this man who is dying between his today and his past life?
He is a person who all his life was busy thinking about himself, about his work, about his career, about his women, about his poems. . . .

He is a poet. Is the story based on a real personality?
A poet and author. Very well-known in Greece. But it is not a film about a man who really exists or existed. He is not a real character. He has lost his life because he hadn't learned to recognize that he was not alone. He hasn't realized the real value of the other people in his life, of other people in general.

What did he fail to see?
He didn't understand the meaning of real, genuine contact; he had never taken the time to really see the others, to really recognize them. In the film you see one day from his past life, too.

Then the film consists of two days: a today and a day in the past?
Yes. The two days are intertwined, somehow. You see his relationship with

his women, his relationship to the past, his relationship to the little boy from the traffic light, to today. And then you see a series of goodbyes.

So the border, in this film, is not a physical border. It has nothing to do with the fact that the little boy is a refugee from Albania?
No, no. It is the border between life and death, between those two limits that enclose us.

Is the film or a part of it based on some Greek myth?
Only the fact that we are dealing with an author and a poet, in other words, someone who works with words. In the film Alexander tells the little boy the story of another poet, and that one is a well-known national figure in Greece. Dyonisios Solomos, who was born in Zakhintos but grew up in Italy, and who much later in life had to re-find his Greek. So when he returns from Italy he buys those Greek words he doesn't know, which people bring to him. Because at the age of 22 and his return to his homeland he wants to write his poems in Greek. That was about 1818, when a Greek rebellion against the Turks was in the making, in which he wanted to participate through his poetry, in the romantic way of his epoch. In a small notebook he enters the words he hears. He has this Dante-esque idea to bring about a reunification of the Greek language. For him language meant freedom. Not like Heidegger, who said that language was our home. Solomos tried to write in a form of Greek from which all Greek poetry after him is derived, as Dante did with Italian. At that time it was not [considered seemly] to write in the language of the simple people.

Poetry was elitist?
Yes, exactly. And Solomos tried to fight this notion and is today considered a renewer. At the time it was usual to write in a Greek that today we call "Katarevusa." Solomos wrote in what we now call "Demotiki," the language of the people.

And how does this story enter into the film?
I have somewhat enlarged the story, pushed it a little. When I was writing this story into my script, I thought this was the real story of that poet. Namely, that he gave to everyone who brought him a word he didn't know, some remuneration, so that he sort of bought the words. It was said that

poor people often came to him to sell him words. I was so sure of these facts that I told the story of how I had put them in my script to a Solomist, an expert on Solomos's work. He was aghast: the story wasn't true at all. "Where did you get this crazy idea?" he said. I didn't remember where I had heard it. While it is true that he collected the language of the people, it is not true that he actually paid for words. So that must have evolved in my imagination, and since it seemed to me to be a very poetic idea, I left it in.

How did you get all this into the story of Alexander?
The little boy, when he sees that Alexander is sad, in order to comfort him brings him words he has picked up himself. He goes out into the crowd and every time comes back with a new word. He says the word to Alexander, and Alexander pays him something for it. That becomes like a game between them. And among these words there are three, with which he is left at the end of the film, words that actually express the essence of the film, as if his whole life was reflected in these three words. The three words are *korfulamu*—that's a delicate word, and the exact translation of it is something like "heart of a flower," but in Greece the word is used to express the feeling of a child when it sleeps in the arms of its mother. It's a kind of grandmother-word, which by chance I picked up myself, here in Thessaloniki, on the beach.

And the other words?
The second word I got from an old seaman, a Pirot, who brought the word to me. It's a word that has been totally forgotten today, *xenitis,* which derives from the root for strangeness, and it means a stranger, but a stranger who is a stranger everywhere. *Xenos* is the word for stranger, but *xenitis* is the one who finds himself in the situation of being a stranger, and it describes the feeling of being a stranger. Or a feeling of exile.

These then are words that accompany the path of his life. With which word does the film end?
The third word is *argathini,* and that means "very late at night." Those are the three words Alexander finds in the course of his game with the boy, and which at the same time somehow comment on the life he has lived. They are the three words the boy leaves with him when he goes away. They stand for his path, they summarize his life.

Do you mean to say that in life we always remain strangers to ourselves?
Not necessarily to ourselves, but somehow, yes. For example, I feel somehow like a stranger in Greece. I live here in a situation that is as if my house wasn't here, as if this wasn't my home. It comes back to the words spoken by Mastroianni in my film *The Suspended Step of the Stork* (*To Meteoro Vima Tou Pelargou*, '91): We have crossed the border but we are still here. . . . How many borders do you have to cross to arrive at home?

In your films there are often scenes where people are separated by a river, and each one stays on his side. Often, anyway.
Mainly in my last three films.

Is that because you yourself feel that you are more and more pushed into a situation such as expressed by Mastroianni in [The Suspended Step]?
I think that I feel more and more that I am a man who has ceased to understand it all. On the other hand I do not feel that I am being misunderstood, and that is very important. I would be ashamed to maintain that. There simply are more and more things which I do not understand, only I. But I continue to try and understand, even in cases where I see that others have stopped trying. Or in instances where others find that understanding is simple. For me the deeper understanding of things is becoming ever more difficult. That is my work as a filmmaker: you make a film in order to perceive with greater clarity what it is that is not clear in your consciousness.

Is that how you start?
Yes.

So again we can say that all of your work is a search?
Yes, that's why they are always voyages. Even if a film, like this one, takes place in a single city. For me, every film is a voyage, everything is voyage, search. Knowledge comes to me during the voyage. I think that during my voyages I have managed to understand certain things that without voyaging—in this extended sense—I would never have understood. So in the end, after all, I believe I have understood quite a lot.

Do you think that during your life's voyage you have always understood things better, or ever more things less well? What increases, knowledge, compassion, or perplexity?

It depends on the theme. If you were to talk to me about politics, for example, I would have to tell you that I understand less all the time and in the end I understand nothing. By the way, I think that's the case for most people. Or at least it's the case of many. But if you were to speak to me about human relations, there is nothing to understand or not to understand. Things are the way they are. You have to accept human relations as you find them. With their weaknesses, their moments of joy, their moments of pain. The only thing you learn, probably, is the regret that in certain moments you didn't let yourself go more.

We are taught as children never to let ourselves go. . . .
Exactly. I think that form of education robs us of our *souplesse*, our adaptability to life. We become too rigid. Too rigid for life the way it really is. We fight it with the wrong methods, the wrong self-protection. We are full of drawers—"my childhood," "my youth"—and in order to get rid of those drawers in our soul we need time, a lot of time. Apart from the things that come towards you and which you do not have the time to taste. Things which thus are lost to you. And maybe it is often the most important things which, in this way, are lost to you.

Of your three words, two are an expression of feeling, the warmth of the mother and the fact that one always feels a stranger in life. What is the emotion expressed by argathini, *"very late at night"?*
The first word stands for everything that is love, closeness, intimacy, with whoever it may be, your mother or your lover. The second expresses the existential side of the story. The state of the soul. And the third expresses time.

Our enemy?
In my film, time is the central theme. As Heraklitos said: What is time? Time is the small child playing with pebbles on the edge of the sea. *Argathini* here means that time has passed, after the short meeting with the boy, and that it is now important to become aware of this fact. After all, the word itself was also a present from the boy. In the film we also see short, other experiences of the man, and you get the feeling that he consists only of these short experiences (*"des brèves rencontres"*), except for this last, real experience of his life (*"la seule, vraie rencontre"*).

Which has now come to him too late?
Yes, that, too, comes too late. Because both are leaving. There is the goodbye of the boy, who smuggles himself into a container to try and enter the U.S. illegally, and then his own goodbye, at least this consciousness of having to leave definitively.

Does he die at the end of the film?
No, no. He has to enter hospital but he refuses to enter. He thus rejects the "normal" end.

Watching your films one after the other, do you find that there is a common tendency, maybe to more pessimism, or maybe to the contrary?
I really think the evolution is to the contrary, certainly not towards greater pessimism. The fact that my characters do not accept the rational represents the first time that they allow themselves to let go. For the first time he doesn't go in the direction where anybody else would have gone in his stead.

In any case, you do not blame society but the individual.
Politics, you mean? The battle is always the battle of the self, the self against everything that is unusual, unjust and incalculable. The individual must always fight against everything in this life, because there is the illusion that there is a meaning, a goal. But there is no meaning, no usefulness. The battle is life itself. I no longer deal with politics, with generalizations. I have stopped understanding them.

Is filmmaking, then, for you, a form of poetry, in the sense of the "cinema di poesia" of Pasolini, as juxtaposed to the "cinema di prosa" of Antonioni? After all, I see that your deep interest lies in literature and poetry.
That is too large a question. I simply feel that I have been lucky enough to have been able to make the films I wanted to make. Now, at this point in my life, my relationship is only with the things I have made. I expect nothing. Not even from the film itself (to keep quiet about finances—that has always been a drama). When I say I expect nothing, I mean, for example, that I expect no reactions, not from the critics and not from the festivals—not from anybody. I accept the game played around the release, but in essence it doesn't interest me. What develops ever more strongly is my relationship to my work itself and with the possibilities of expression. That is my way, to

seek the words, those few words which can express and contain all that I have done and my life itself, and which will be the words I shall leave behind one day.

Are you making the films for somebody?
I recommend to you the very well-known formula of Borges, who said, "I write for myself, for my friends, however few or many they may be, and to pass the time that flows by."

The Time of His Life: *Eternity and a Day*

GEOFF ANDREW/1998

IN THE 1994 EDITION of his much-lauded *Biographical Dictionary of Film*, the critic David Thomson argued that the Greek filmmaker Theo Angelopoulos should be counted among the handful of truly great masters still working in the cinema. That was a year before his epic Balkan odyssey *Ulysses' Gaze* won the Grand Jury Prize in Cannes, and four years before *Eternity and a Day* deservedly won the Palme d'Or. Yet Angelopoulos's relative obscurity outside the festival circuit endures. True, most screenings for last year's Riverside retrospective sold out, but he's still widely perceived—by those unfamiliar with his work—as a "difficult" filmmaker. Not that his movies are inaccessible in terms of their stories, which exude the simplicity of myth. Rather, one suspects, it's the combination of their stately pace (jokes abound about *Eternity and a Day* being the running time), provenance (Greece isn't known as a great filmmaking nation), and abiding, unfashionable fascination with big themes—life and death, memory and regret, history and identity, art and alienation—that puts off punters whose expectations are more attuned to the wham-bam aesthetics of the contemporary mainstream. That's a pity, because Thomson's right: cast aside prejudice, and Angelopoulos's blend of classicism and modernism casts a mesmerizing spell almost unique in today's cinema.

The key to his work, thematically and stylistically, is his distinctive handling of time and place. Increasingly, since winning international acclaim with 1975's magisterial *The Travelling Players* (scheduled for revival this summer), Angelopoulos has structured most of his films as journeys, at once physical and spiritual, geographical and temporal. Accordingly, the defining characteristic of his style is the "travelling shot": in long, fluid takes (the complexity of which can often make, say, the oft-quoted entry into the Copacabana Club in *GoodFellas* seem unambitiously straightforward), the protagonist, like the camera, passes through space *and* time, as characters and events recalled from the past, or indeed from private fantasy, invade the reality of the present. The result is dreamlike, often exhilarating (the gliding camera movements, immaculate compositions and lyrical use of color make Angelopoulos's cameraman Giorgos Arvanitis a near-genius in his own right), and immediately recognizable as the signature of a supremely assured, imaginative *poet* of the cinema. Which is why it's tempting to see *Eternity and a Day*—about an ailing writer recalling happier times and meeting a young refugee from Albania when he leaves the family home to face an uncertain, all-too-brief future—as partly autobiographical.

"Well," smiles Angelopoulos, "it's true that the inspiration for the film was that I'm getting older, and friends keep passing away these days. I first had the idea the morning I learned the actor Gian Maria Volonte had died in his hotel room on the shoot of *Ulysses Gaze;* I'd spent the day before with him, when he seemed so happy, working on a script he liked, in a place he liked, with people he liked. His death got me wondering: How would it be for a man aware that the next day he'll no longer exist? How does he wake up, drink his coffee, where does he go, what does he do, when facing that frontier?

"Then, after a few months of thinking along those lines, another idea came up: the broken lives of the abandoned children, victims of the Balkan War, whom I'd met while making *Gaze*. I also wanted to do something about a poet, and language, reflecting Heidegger's idea that our identity is inextricably tied up with our mother tongue. Then, when I went to visit Tonino Guerra [regular collaborator on Angelopoulos's scripts], I realized I had not three subjects but just one. So we spent a long while in discussion, like those ancient "peripatetic" philosophers who always walked about as they argued, and put the story together."

Appropriately but tragically, illness and death have haunted Angelopoulos's films of late; besides Volonte's untimely demise during *Gaze,* he was also robbed of Marcello Mastroianni, the lead in his earlier *The Beekeeper* and *The Suspended Step of the Stork* and the original choice to play Alexander, the writer in the new film. "But when I went to see him," says Angelopoulos with a sigh, "he was too sick. He'd always been so full of life, but here was a ghost; it was like foreseeing his death, and after what happened with Volonte, I just thought: This is impossible. So then I called Jean-Louis Trintignant, who was so nervous about the situation he couldn't make up his mind, and then I thought of several other actors, some of them English—but there's always that language problem with me. [Angelopoulos's English is minimal; our interview is conducted in French.] Then someone mentioned Bruno Ganz. I knew he's a very good actor and speaks lots of languages, like all Swiss, but I was thinking of him in Wenders's film, where he was young, looked very open, and not at all Southern European! So I didn't know what to do. Then in Paris I met up with Ganz, and when I saw him, he was wearing a long grey overcoat, had a grey beard, and looked so old as he does in my film. So we changed nothing . . . including the overcoat."

Like all his films, *Eternity and a Day* (the title paraphrases Orlando's claim, in *As You Like It,* that his love will last "For ever and a day") merges the personal and political: not only do Alexander's memories of family life find him revisiting key moments in recent Greek history and pondering the story of Solomos, the poet who wrote the national anthem and unified the modern Greek language, but his meeting with the Albanian orphan reflects on the current turmoil in the Balkans. The resulting mix is at once specific and universal in its relevance.

"Absolutely; that's my intention, anyway. I can't be indifferent to what happens around me, like what's happening in Kosovo. [This interview took place last June.] And of course I am very Greek in my concerns: every artist is deeply affected by where he's lived, so his work can become kind of a spiritual autobiography. The books we read, people we meet, our childhood and adolescence—our most important years, to my mind—all work their way into our films, as do things like war. During the Greek Civil War, not only was my family divided into Communists and anti-Communists, but my father was imprisoned and condemned to death; when I was nine, my mother took me into a room full of corpses to identify his body. How could I not be deeply marked by that, as I am by all the moments of happiness and sadness, the language, the landscape, and so on?

"So yes, there are always references to historical and contemporary reality, but I try to show it from a poetic viewpoint. Other filmmakers might make more realist films, and I respect that, but that's not my way of seeing things."

Hence, *Eternity and a Day* is no dry ideological tract but a lyrical, metaphorical response to the anxieties of an era: the orphan, for instance, is not merely a refugee, but a reflection of Alexander's own youth and an angel of death who guides him through the tangled labyrinth of past and present, allowing him to come to terms with the fact that his vocation often led him to neglect his family. Does this last aspect of the film reflect Angelopoulos's own ambivalence towards creative life? He laughs.

"Well, the Spanish writer Jorge Semprun recently published a book entitled *To Live or to Write* . . . ! When I'm at home, my daughter says, "Yes, we know, you're off again tomorrow, you're doing this and that, we never see you." Suddenly I find she's grown up, a woman; that I missed out on discovering certain things with her. Those lost moments are the price we pay for creativity, and that can make me sad.

"Every time I make a film, I say it might be my last, but then. . . . It's like two old men at a café. It's spring. They're watching the world go by, especially beautiful women. They watch one walk off into the distance. One guy says, 'How long do we do this?' And his friend replies, 'Until the end.' For me, it's like that with cinema."

I Shoot the Way I Breathe: *Eternity and a Day*

GABRIELLE SCHULZ/1998

Q: *I have the impression that your last movie* Eternity and a Day *is more emotional and personal than the ones before. Is this movie more autobiographical?*
A: All my movies are part and expression of my biography and my life. The experiences I have made and the dreams I have had. Some of them are closer to my intellectual occupations, others to events in my real life. There are words and sentences I have read here and there. *Eternity and a Day* is not more autobiographical than all my other movies, but it is more personal because I gave more expression to my feelings than to my thoughts. The autobiographical aspect is probably more in evidence, because all my recent films have dealt with artists and crises in the creative process. I think it is not as intellectual as my other films. If you insist, I would say that everything I did after *Megalexandros* is autobiographical to a certain degree, starting with *Voyage to Cythera*. As a matter of fact, I would divide the six films I have made since in two separate trilogies. For me, *Voyage to Cythera* represents the Silence of History. *The Beekeeper* is the Silence of Love and, *Landscape in the Mist* is the Silence of God. In *Landscape in the Mist* the little boy asks his sister at one point: "What is the meaning of borders?" In the next three films, I tried to find an answer to his question. *The Suspended Step of the Stork* deals with geographical borders separating countries and people. *Ulysses' Gaze* talks about the borders, or one could say the limits, of human vision. *Eternity and a Day* discusses the borders between life and death.

Excerpts published in *Die Zeit*, February 1999. © 1998 by Gabrielle Schulz. Reprinted by permission.

Q: *In this film, your protagonist, the poet Alexander, is in a deep crisis. He has to leave his house by the sea where he has lived his whole life. He is seriously ill and knows that he may not survive the surgical intervention for which he is entering the hospital the next day. In this situation he meets a little Albanian boy and undertakes a journey with him through the key moments of his life. Can you describe the inner conflict of Alexander?*

A: The whole movie is a continuous journey through time, through the present and the past. There are no distinct borders between reality and imagination; the borders are fluid. Alexander's journey starts in reality. He saves the boy from the clutches of an organization specializing in selling children for adoption to well-to-do families. But at a certain point in time the journey becomes an inner one. For example, when the two reach the Albanian frontier. You remember the sequence in the fog; there are people hanging on the wire fence. Of course, the frontier does not look like this. All these incidents and images only occur in Alexander's imagination. It is a fantasy. The border with this threatening wire fence is a frontier in Alexander himself. The boy only helps him to face his inner conflict, and the boy gives Alexander a reason to travel through the key moments of his life, to remember the happy moments he had with his late wife Anna.

Q: *In a monologue Alexander says: "I regret that I have never finished anything." Were you talking about yourself in this monologue?*

A: I must admit I have never finished anything the way I have wanted to. There have always been barriers, physical and emotional ones, that have prevented me from reaching a state of overall satisfaction. From a superficial point of view, Alexander seems to be a human being who never finishes anything, but when he starts looking inside himself he finds out that his ambitions have always been bigger than the results he has obtained. I could say the same about me.

Q: *You said before that for you, this film is about the borders between life and death. But one could say the same thing about* The Beekeeper.

A: It is not at all the same thing. In *The Beekeeper* the protagonist decides he is going to die. In *Eternity and a Day* Alexander hopes to find a bridge that will allow him to transcend death, and that bridge, he believes, are the words that will keep him alive, whether he will physically cease to exist or not.

Q: *What meaning does time itself have for you?*
A: Time is a child who plays with stones on a beach. The characters of my film travel through time and space as if time and space do not exist. The most important question is: "How long will tomorrow last?" And the answer is "Eternity and a Day." If we are lucky, we may live up to the image of the future, which we carry with us, today.

Q: *The casting in this film. How did you decide on Bruno Ganz and how did you find the boy, Achilleas Skevis?*
A: Originally, the person I had in mind for the part, once the script was finished, was Marcello Mastroianni. We were very close since the day we started working together in *The Beekeeper*. He had been terribly disappointed not to play in *Ulysses' Gaze* and he seemed to be ideal for the part. Then, when I met him in Italy, where he was playing on stage, I realized his health was so poor that he would be never able to do it. I couldn't tell him that, so finally, he was the one to say it. It was the last time I saw him. He died soon after that. I saw Ganz on stage in Paris playing Ulysses, and I somehow felt it was an omen. More so, since he looked exactly the way I had visualized the part. As for the boy, I had told the people I work with that I would like to find someone who had been subject to similar experiences. We tested many boys, but somehow, when Achilleas walked in, I knew I had the right one. And indeed, he proved to be not only the perfect choice but also a real pro all through the production of this film.

Q: *Don't you have a problem with actors who do not speak Greek yet play Greek characters, like Ganz in this film?*
A: With Mastroianni it was relatively easy. He always insisted on having his own voice on the soundtrack, and he learned how to pronounce the Greek dialog. With Harvey Keitel it was more complicated, but at least, the character in *Ulysses' Gaze* had an excuse; he had been many years in America and therefore could use English most of the time. Ganz spoke German on the shoot—it is the language he is most comfortable with—and we had to use a Greek actor to dub him. The truth is I am still uneasy when I hear someone else's voice coming out from his mouth.

Q: *There is one specific sequence from your past movies I particularly remember. It is the moment in* Landscape in the Mist *when the little girl says, "I am afraid."*

"Don't be afraid," answers the boy, "I am going to tell you a story. In the beginning there was chaos and then light broke through." The fog dissolves, the horizon appears and the children embrace the trunk of a tree. Are you trying to bring, through your films, some light into the chaos?

A: Yes, this is the reason I make movies. I am not a missionary. I don't want to educate people; I try to find a way from chaos to light. We live in confused times where values do not exist any longer. Melancholy goes along with confusion and disorientation. But the questions people ask themselves are still the same. Where do I come from, where do I go? Questions about life, death, love, friendship, youth, and age.

Originally, the end of the scene you have described was much more pessimistic. I wanted the children to disappear in the fog. But one of my daughters, who had read the script, asked me: Where is the father of the children? Where is their home? So I overworked the script and created a more optimistic end. During their journey the two children undergo a deep initiation, and they learn to believe in their own world. They also learn to see things that are not visible at first sight.

Anyway, I am equally pessimistic and optimistic about our abilities to find ways out of the confusion of time. But I deeply wish that people would learn to dream again. Nothing is more real than our dreams.

Q: *Greece's landscape seems to be a central motif in your films. You seem to measure physical landscapes like a topographer and then use them to expose through them the emotional landscapes of your characters.*

A: I have been asked again and again by Greeks: Where are these landscapes? In fact, the landscapes you see in my films do not exist. True, some parts are real. I have been travelling much through Greece. On these journeys I discovered elements which fascinated me—a house, a street, a hill, a village. I put all these single elements together in a collage. Sometimes it's the colors, sometimes the shapes that go well together. In a certain way I create images like a painter, thus projecting my vision on a canvas. I do not pretend to describe reality; I create my own vision that I project on reality. The result is something in-between. The question I am asking myself all the time is: How can I transform personal experiences into poetry?

Q: *Since you mention poetry, you have in* Eternity and a Day *the marvelous story of the nineteenth-century poet Dyonisios Solomos, who went around Greece and bought words for his poems. Is it a true story?*

A: Partly. Solomos was a great poet, the son of an aristocrat from the Ionian islands, greatly influenced at the time by Italian culture, and a lowly maid. His father, wishing to cut off his proletarian roots, sent him away when he was just a boy, nine or ten years old, to be educated in an Italian convent. He grew up there, almost finished his studies, and was already writing poetry in Italian when he found out about the Greek uprising against the Turks, who were the masters of the Balkan peninsula at that time. Memories of his childhood, the image of his mother and the songs she used to sing to him, came back to him, and he decided to return to his homeland and participate in the national struggle. But, being a poet, what could he do, except write? He felt he should write revolutionary poems, lament the death of heroes, and evoke the forgotten image of freedom. Since his knowledge of Greek was very limited, he went out, roaming around the country, collecting words he had never heard before and dutifully writing them all up in his notebook. That is as far as the factual truth goes. The notion of paying for every new word he acquired was my own invention. The metaphor is clear. Our mother tongue is our only real identity card. To quote Heidegger: our only home is our language. Every word opens new doors for the person who acquires it, but to go through that door, you have to pay.

Q: *There are magic, unforgettable moments in each one of your films, which stand out and take one's breath away. In this film, it is the bus ride, at night, in the rain, through Thessaloniki.*
A: This sequence was completely different in the script. What you see on the screen is the result of improvisation on the set. Originally, it was supposed to be a very realistic sequence, both the image and the sound. But as I was shooting it, I sense that I should convey here a feeling of time standing still. Which is the reason the original scene was changed.

Q: *All through the film, one finds images that are familiar from your previous movies. The yellow parkas, the mountain landscape at the border, and so on.*
A: This is of course intentional. These are images that belong to my own personal imagery. I believe that every film director who has a distinct identity possesses his own set of images that represent him—the use of certain colors, style mannerisms, things that are repeated from one film to another.

Q: *Journeys and homecomings are very frequent in your films. What do they mean to you?*

A: Journeys provoke changes, initiations. You get to know yourself better. When I travel, I travel through my inner world. My motivation to travel also expresses my wish to come home again.

Q: *Is Greece your home? Or do you feel like Alexander, who says about himself that he had lived his whole life in exile?*
A: In Greece I feel like a stranger who is still seeking for his own home. I have always felt like this and I don't know why. I have been crossing borders inside myself again and again. And the question is still there: How many more borders do I have to cross before I reach my goal. Although I feel like a stranger in Greece, I cannot leave this country. I would feel the same way anywhere else.

Q: *You said once: I shoot like I breathe. How do you breathe?*
A: I don't force anything when shooting. I try hard to give space to the time and time to the space. I allow time to breathe during the shooting.

Q: *Can you understand why you were given a Golden Palm, Cannes's supreme award, for* Eternity and a Day *and not for* Ulysses' Gaze?
A: Getting the Palm is like having a date with a woman. Ulysses and me, we were at the date, but the Palm did not show up. This time the Palm came, probably because I did not expect it.

. . . And about All the Rest

DAN FAINARU/1999

Q: *Your parents are from the South, the Peloponesus and Crete. And yet you seem to be obsessed with the North, with dark skies, cold winters, heavy rains.*
A: It's a question I am often asked. I have no explanation. I have often tried in the past to find one, but couldn't really. Maybe one has to look far back; a psychoanalyst might unveil the real sources. What I can tell you is that when I set out to make my first feature film, *Reconstruction*, I remember one afternoon, in the small village where the story took place. The landscape was all shades of gray, the dark sky, the drab little houses, the stony hills. It was raining, just a drizzle; a thin fog was covering the mountain, and the village was practically deserted. Most people had gone to Germany like so many other Greeks in the fifties, in search of a better life. Only a few old women dressed in black, barely visible in the gloomy light, sneaked silently through the narrow streets. Suddenly I heard an old, cracked voice, singing a very old song. It was an ancient old man, singing "Oh, little lemon tree . . . Oh, little lemon tree . . . ," the song I finally used in the film. It was a magic moment which marked me for life: the rain, the fog, the gray stones, the women in black looking like ghosts, and the old man singing. This deserted village, a forgotten corner in a land ruled by military dictatorship, was for me the image of a country drained out by the constant flow of departing emigrants, and the only thing left in it is an old love song. This image has probably imprinted itself in my subconscious, the matrix for all the films to follow. This is the reason I believe the first film is the original seed. Everything that

---

Interview first published in this book. © 1999 Dan Fainaru.

comes later is either a variation, a development, or an elaboration evolving from that first theme. For me, *Reconstruction* contains all the themes I later developed. I really think one always does the same film, over and over again. Lately I watched again a number of Bergman films, and this is true for him as well.

Q: *Was it at home, from your parents, that you first acquired the love for culture?*
A: Not really. My father was a shopkeeper, my mother was a simple housewife mostly concerned with the well-being of her children. I don't remember the origins, but I know I started writing for the first time during the civil war, in Athens, towards the end of 1944, a period we still call "The Red December." The communists, who suspected him of being a liberal, arrested my father. As a matter of fact, the person who arrested him was my own cousin, because you have to know that my family—like the rest of the country—was divided in two, part liberal and part communist. During my father's absence, for reasons that are still not very clear to me, I wrote my first poems. And since that time, I sincerely believe that poetry was the foremost influence in my life. My original masters were poets, and if, at first, my writing was a bit childish, by the time I was sixteen, I actually had some of my poems published in literary magazines and in cultural supplements of daily newspapers. Writing poetry was my first artistic activity.

Q: *Do you still write poetry?*
A: Yes, I do. But going back to your question. I loved music, but I could not afford to buy tickets for the Sunday concerts of the national orchestra. Instead I was glued every Sunday morning to the radio, listening to their broadcasts. So, you see, there is no one definite answer to your question; I can only tell you there was no real preoccupation with culture in our family. It's true that many years later, I found in one of my father's trunks books he had kept from his youth. Among them I discovered Zweig and Balzac, more classics of all kinds. So it seems that in his youth, this shopkeeper was interested in other things besides commerce.

As I told you, one day he was arrested and disappeared. He was away for a few months, kept somewhere in the center of Greece, and once he was released, he had to walk all the way home, half the length of the country. I remember seeing him at the end of the street, at the time children were still playing in the street, walking slowly towards us. I rushed home and called my mother. We knew he was supposed to come home, but when I told her I'd seen him, she rushed into the street to greet him. Once back inside, we were in such a state, no one could utter a single word. We sat around the table, drank our soup looking at each other in silence. We all felt like crying but kept back our tears. This is, as you may remember, the opening scene of *Reconstruction*.

Q: *Do you remember anything of the German occupation?*
A: I have said it often enough—I am a war child. When I was born, Greece was ruled by a dictator, General Metaxas. In 1940, the Italians invaded Greece. The first sound I remember is that of the war sirens. And the first image is that of Germans entering Athens, just as I painted it in the opening sequence of *Voyage to Cythera*. It's all there, including the episode of the young German soldier directing traffic, the child touching his shoulder, and then running away into a maze of narrow streets with the soldier chasing him. One way or another, I have the feeling that we always dip into our own reservoir of memories and relive certain episodes we have experienced in real life. My work is full of all those special moments of my childhood and adolescence, my emotions and dreams at that time. I believe the one source for everything we do is there.

Q: *When did you first take on a distinct political stand?*
A: As long as I was in Greece, I considered myself apolitical. Only when I got to Paris did I choose, consciously, to join the Left. Of course, in the fifties, I took part in all sorts of student demonstrations, for instance to support Cyprus, but there was no political conscience behind it. I stayed away whenever left-wing and right-wing students would fight on the campus. At the same time, that is after I graduated high school, I was beginning to realize that my interest in cinema was gradually growing almost into an obsession. I was frequenting all-day cinemas showing detective stories of which I saw a lot. Naturally, the American classics of the genre—Huston, Polonski, Hawks, Walsh—figured at the top of the list. But the first film I ever saw was Michael Curtiz's *Angels with Dirty Faces*. I still remember the scene where James Cagney is taken to the electric chair, the shadows on the wall, his scream: "I don't want to die." I must have been nine or ten at the time. This may explain my fascination to this day with detective stories, be they novels or films.

Q: *Is it only films you were becoming interested in or also literature, music, painting, and the rest of the arts?*
A: Less in painting, more in literature and music. And in literature, I preferred poetry to novels, though I must have read, my God, practically anything that was translated at the time in Greek. Later, I started reading in French as well.

Q: *Did you have favorites?*
A: Dostoyevski. Sometimes I would pretend to be sick and stayed home just to read *The Brothers Karamazov*. Also Tolstoi, Chekhov, all the Russian literature. I don't know whether it was the fashion or not, but it left on me an indelible impression. And of course Stendhal, *La Chartreuse de Parme, Le Rouge et le Noir*. Of all French writers, I felt closest to Stendhal. Only later, did I discover Sartre and Camus.

Q: *Are these still your favorites?*
A: Stendhal, yes. Dostoyevski, of course.

Q: *And in music?*
A: I started with Mozart, like everyone else—he is the most accessible—then I went through all the composers and finally came to rest with Bach and Vivaldi.

Q: *You studied law, you were about to graduate, and all of a sudden you dropped everything. Why?*
A: True, I was about to graduate when I made up my mind that I did not want to become a lawyer. I had my doubts before, but then I reached the point where I had to make a decision, knowing I would have all my family against me. My uncle was a lawyer, he had his own office and no heirs, and everything was ready for me to take over. And there I was, turning my back on it all. But I must mention one other thing. I believe the event that marked me at the time more than anything else was the death of my sister at the age of eleven. If not for that event, I might have well pursued the path that had been lined up for me. For until that moment, our family was a normal one. After the tragedy, a veil of gloom descended over our home. My mother cried her eyes out for months; she went on mourning for years.

It is also true that when I started frequenting the cinema, unlike my

friends who noticed mainly the stars, Errol Flynn, Tyrone Power, Ava Gardner, I always paid attention to the name of the person who signed the film, the director. Not that I was doing it consciously, but it was the author of the film that attracted me. Sure enough, most of the films were American. There were many great detective stories, but there were also marvelous musicals and of course the films of Elia Kazan. There is a public debate now in Greece concerning those films. Most people claim he is a great filmmaker but. . . .
He has betrayed, maybe not without justification, but he went way too far in this treason. It is only natural that men like Jules Dassin, who have been the victims of his acts, refuse to forget and forgive. Which does not detract from Kazan's talent as a director or the quality of the films he made at the time.

Q: *Did you follow the cinema press at the time?*
A: The first interesting film magazine in Greece appeared when I was already a student at the University. The New Wave emerged at the time with the first films of Resnais and Godard. I saw *Breathless* in a commercial cinema, presented as just another police yarn. The thing that fascinated me was his way of turning upside down all accepted cinema codes.

What I am trying to tell you is that gradually, certainly without meaning to, I was being drawn closer to the cinema and losing interest in whatever was going on at the University. I tried to enroll in a cinema course, but I was very shy then and disliked the atmosphere I found in that course. I was already reading everything published on cinema that I could get my hands on, like Georges Sadoul's lexicons and his history of cinema, which had been translated in Greek. When my father fell ill, I used it as an excuse to withdraw from school and do my military service. The two years I served in uniform were particularly interesting as far as I am concerned, because I was detached to a small drafting commission travelling all through Greece to check the new recruits. I was the assistant of the Army MD, and it was a chance for me to go from one end of Greece to the other for the first time in my life. All I knew before that was just Athens, where I was born. I had plenty of time to read, to write, and to prepare my departure.

Q: *Had you already made up your mind what you would like to do, if not law?*
A: For me, it was perfectly clear that I wanted to make films. When I was released from the army, I got my friends together, told them I wanted to go and study in Paris, but that I had no money. Each one of them put in a small

contribution, just enough for a train ticket. I left without a penny, but luckily, I met someone on the train who told me that I could stay the night at his uncle's, for one night only. Next day, I went to an address given to me by my French teacher in Athens. It was outside Paris, some ten kilometers away from the nearest underground station, a small house he used to live in before going to Athens. Once I settled there, I went first to the Alliance Française to improve my French a bit; then I looked for work, like all other students. Night porter in a hotel, selling carpets—I even sang in a Greek nightclub. Anything that came my way. Then a Greek diplomat who had read some of my poems found me a job and helped me find lodgings in the Cité Universitaire. Officially, I studied literature, but my real purpose was to study film.

Q: *And of course you went to study at the world-famous IDHEC (Institut de Hautes Etudes Cinématographiques) but never graduated.*
A: That's true, they kicked me out at the end of the first year, claiming I lacked discipline.

Q: *What did that mean, exactly?*
A: I was accepted at the IDHEC despite the fact that my grades in physics and math were not brilliant. On the other hand they were the highest in history, art, literature, etc. When we began shooting our first shorts, the entire class was persuaded my films were by far the best. "The new Resnais" and other compliments of this kind rather went to my head. I behaved as though I was already a certified filmmaker but the teachers did not like this attitude very much. They expected us all to follow certain procedures in our work, which I found totally superfluous. One day, we were asked to prepare the shooting script for a short subject. That morning, I came in late, entered the classroom, apologized for not being on time, and then asked whether anyone had a cigarette for me. Everybody froze, because at the time it was strictly forbidden to smoke in class. Someone hesitantly offered a cigarette, I lit it up, took the chalk in my hand, and drew a circle on the blackboard. The teacher looked at me and asked: "What is this?" I told him: "This is my shooting script." "What do you mean?" he asked, and I explained: "It's a 360-degree panoramic shot." He looked at me sternly and said, "I believe the purpose of your presence here is to learn." "Not at all," I replied, "the purpose of my being here is to experiment. If you cannot do this in school, where can you do it?" Furious, he told me: "You better go back and sell your

genius in Greece." I left the room, and later, I was told he went to the director and threatened, "It's either him or me." I did make a second short, and when it was screened, the entire class stood up and cheered. But the lecturer was adamant: "I know it's not the film you are applauding, it's me you're booing." Then the director called me into his office and told me that I was "too mature for the school." "I understand you want to make your first films very quickly. Of course you cannot stay with us, but let me give you a piece of free advice. Do not start with a feature film, try a short first." When I left, there were a number of people who protested, people like Georges Sadoul, who taught there and considered me their favorite student, and of course many of the students joined them. But to no avail.

I switched to a course at the Musee de L'Homme under Jean Rouch, who was trying to train people in the techniques of the Cinéma Vérité, the documentary genre he has become famous for, and I even did a number of documentaries there. They used to teach us how to use a handheld camera, how to breathe when shooting with it, how to stand with it, how to stand with your knees slightly bent. We had to train in front of a mirror, to check we were doing everything right. I must say it was rather interesting. Then I decided to do a film on my own. I approached several of my former IDHEC colleagues, each specializing in one of the technical classes, found another friend who had some money to buy the film stock, and together we all set out to make the film, called *Black and White*. It was naturally in black and white, on 16 mm, the story of someone who is being chased all over Paris.

Q: *A detective story already.*
A: Indeed. For what reason is this character on the run, or who chases him, it is never clear. A man alone, threatened by someone or something, we never know what. We shot all over Paris, but then we realized we did not have the money to develop the working print. I never saw what was on that print. Many years later I met two of my friends again. The cameraman who had shot the film, Michel Andrieu, had become in the meantime a film director in his own right. My assistant, who had provided the funds to buy the raw material, had since started adapting foreign films into French and had just finished working on *Ulysses' Gaze*. We were reminiscing about the past when Andrieu told me he had the working print at home. He had retrieved it when he had some money and kept it at home in his garage. It's a bit like

the story of *Ulysses' Gaze,* looking for a piece of film shot at the beginning of the century. I had just found a film I had shot at my beginnings.

Q: *I understand that you already had in mind your very personal film style, particularly the very long camera movements, even at that early stage. What made you decide this is the right kind of cinema for you?*
A: I really don't know. It is true that for a brief while I worked as an usher at the French Cinématheque, not only to make some much-needed money but also to see the films they were screening there. And I think I saw everything that was on their program during that period. Not only the archive films but also previews of new films. Briefly, all the history of cinema. My preferences were established almost automatically. Not in the direction of filmmakers like Eisenstein but rather like Murnau, be it *The Last Laugh* or *Sunrise,* of Orson Welles and his cutting into the camera, or Renoir and his use of deep focus and parallel stories, and of course, Dreyer's *Ordet.* Also the Mizoguchi of *Ugetsu Monogatari.* I remember seeing many of his films without subtitles, just watching the image. And then there was Antonioni, the considerable length of his shots, which went on just a bit longer than expected to allow for a deep breath before going on. I simply felt much more comfortable with this kind of cinema than with any other. Cutting real time into small time pieces, focusing only on the climax of each piece and eliminating the breath at the beginning and the end of each shot, this, in my eyes, was a bit like raping your audience, forcing yourself on it. The logical explanation for this preference of mine came later, but I could feel it in my bones already then. The first shots I ever took were already sequence shots.

Q: *Still, some of the directors you mentioned, like Orson Welles for instance, made extensive use of montage.*
A: Yes, but not always. The Welles I love is that of *The Magnificent Ambersons,* or the opening shot in *Touch of Evil.* As a spectator, I have no problem seeing the films of someone like Kubrick, but as a filmmaker, my preferences lie elsewhere.

Q: *You realize of course that many people associate this style with Miklós Jancsó.*
A: Yes, but he came later. And it is true that he was using sequence shots too, but he did it in a different manner. I saw his first films at the Cinéma-

theque as well, but later, shortly before leaving Paris. Jancsó is someone I like indeed, but his use of the sequence shot is different from mine.

Q: *You used to speak during that period quite often of your predilection for "Brechtian alienation."*
A: Yes. He was everybody's point of reference, at the time. The political cinema was emerging then, and Brecht showed us the way not only to make political films, but to make them politically. That is, to go one step further than the militant pamphlet. To express our opinions but at the same time to keep them in perspective, never forgetting to review them from a critical point of view. Which I felt was very important, though it is not always that evident in the structure of my first film, *Reconstruction*. It begins with the end of the story and ends with the beginning. That and more. The film shows the police reconstructing a murder for the purpose of identifying the culprit, but there is a second reconstruction, that of the media trying to unearth all the juicy titbits that will sell newspapers. Finally, the filmmaker [played by Angelopoulos in person, D. F.] embarks on an attempted reconstruction of his own, trying to reveal the secret reasons behind the killing. At the same time, he reminds the audience that, not being himself a peasant, there is an unbridgeable gap between him and the characters he deals with, and it is his duty to stress this fact time and again. These three versions of the murder complement each other, but all three finally lead us to a locked door, and no key to it. The point of the film is not to find out who the murderer is—we know that from the very beginning. It is about what really happened behind that closed door we see at the end of the film through the camera that is not allowed to go in. The film is about the state of mind and spirit of the entire country at that moment, but it is also, indirectly, a political film made in a political fashion.

The Days of '36 follows the same direction. There is no hero, the main character is in a prison cell and is rarely seen, and the entire action evolves around this cell, as if the subject was the inside of the cell. All dialogues are whispered, murmured, there is no clear, outright statement. Since, in any case, I wouldn't have been allowed to make a film about military dictatorship, I had to use Brecht's formulas for making a political picture despite censorship. The result was a different kind of cinema language, almost an esthetic concept, of speaking in a roundabout way, which may seem at first mysterious and yet is perfectly clear to understand. My Brechtian period came, of course, to an end with *The Travelling Players*.

Q: *Your return from Paris to Greece, was it because you had decided not to make films in France?*

A: After the Jean Rouch course and that first unfinished film, I returned to Athens to see my family. But I also had to meet an Austrian girl with whom I had an affair. She lived in Zurich, she was an air stewardess. We got carried away and decided, on the spur of the moment, to get married. We were supposed to meet in Athens on a certain day, and since I did not like the idea of biding my time in the city until she came, I joined a few friends, painters, who went to Mikonos for a few days. And, believe it or not, I completely forgot the date of the meeting, the marriage arrangements, everything. Some time later, I found out that she did not show up either. That's how I managed stay out of the danger of being married, the only time it had presented itself to me. Sure enough, I have had a family for a long time, but I am not married.

But coming back to your question. I went back to Paris to decide whether I would remain and work there. I already had a number of options, and there was a distinct possibility to make films and establish my career there. I was offered an assistant director's job, I even played in a number of small films, but had to return to Athens. I am not sure why, I think for family reasons. It was long before the Colonels took over, but the university was already boiling. On my way home from the airport, at a certain point I had to get out of the taxi and walk because the traffic in the center of town was completely blocked. By accident, I found myself in the midst of a student demonstration. The police intervened; they were hitting right and left and beating everybody up, and one of the cops went to work on me. I fell down, my glasses broke, I was bloody all over. I reached home, and I was all shook up. That same evening, a friend of mine, a film director called Tonia Marketaki, called me. Unlike me, she did graduate IDHEC, and she was writing at the time on cinema in a left-wing paper, *Demokratiki Allaghi* [*Democratic Change*]. She asked me about my plans for the future, and suggested, in case I chose to stay in Athens, that I become a film critic for that paper. I surprised myself when I answered on the spot: yes. I suspect it was the result of that day's shock. I decided to stay here and understand what was really happening to my country. Suddenly, the Greece I had forgotten completely as I was planning my career in France became very present in my mind. I could not leave anymore. I remained with that paper for three years, from 1964 until 1967, when, after the military coup, the Colonels sent over the military police to tear down our offices and arrest everyone they found there. Luckily, I was away at the time. While writing there, I was approached by the composer Vangelis (later to become famous with Aphrodite's Child and for the music for *Chariots of Fire*). He and some of his friends were playing in a group called Forminx, the name of an antique wind instrument. An American impresario took a fancy to them and wanted to arrange an American tour, but he needed a film to prepare the market before they came in person. Since they were extremely popular at home, a Greek producer expressed his interest in participating, and I was asked to do the promo film. Of course I agreed. For me it was an opportunity to get some experience under my belt, and in a matter of days I wrote a script, a detective story with plenty, maybe even too much, music in it. The intention was to do something in the spirit of Richard Lester's films with the Beatles. But while I was shooting, the two producers got into an argument, and the American partner packed up and left, possibly because the American response to the projected tour was disappointing. The Greek producer was still interested but expected something far more commercial than anything I had in mind. I refused to give in and wanted to leave, but some friends suggested it would be better for me if I was fired. To prompt the producer, I took forty-two takes of the same shot, and that was all the convincing he needed. We went our separate ways after he paid me, and with this money I later shot my first short.

Q: *I asked you if the choice of coming back to Athens was a conscious one, because of your approach to the Greek landscape. It is of such an overwhelming importance in all your films. You lavish on it so much attention, even in the way you talk about it and describe it, that it is practically impossible to associate you with a non-Greek film. Did you ever feel like doing a film elsewhere?*
A: No, never. It has never tempted me. I did shoot certain sequences of my films in other Balkan countries. The last shot in *Landscape in the Mist* was taken in the Italian mountains. I was approached in the past with offers to shoot in Italy or France, but as time goes by, I feel more bound than ever to my country. I also know what happened to some other filmmakers who tried to work abroad only to discover what an impossible task that is. Antonioni did not really succeed, and neither has my friend Wim Wenders. Now he is working regularly in America, but I prefer the films he shot in Germany. It is

no accident that people like Fellini or Bergman (with rare exceptions) have never left their own country, and no one would claim that Renoir's American films are his best.

Q: *And yet you are sometimes very critical of your homeland.*
A: True. I am certainly very critical at times, but one can be critical of his own family without feeling the need to abandon it. Not to mention the fact that I am very often criticized by my own family, the Greeks.

Q: *In an interview, some years ago, you claimed that for many of the Greek filmmakers, you were the enemy, probably because they were not very comfortable in your shadow. Things must have changed since, haven't they?*
A: My country and myself, we have a kind of love-hate relationship. Sometimes I tend to be very critical, and many of my countrymen believe that I am blocking their way, crushing all the others under my personality, that my presence is suffocating and leaves them no room to grow and develop on their own. It is true that I have been, for the last thirty years, the one to represent Greek cinema on the international scene. That's a long time, several generations, so it is natural that it has generated some bitterness, not only among filmmakers but also among film critics. But this is par for the course, certainly in all smaller countries. I visited Denmark once, after *The Travelling Players,* and the person who distributed my film was gracious enough to ask me whether there were any Danish films I would like to see. I asked for some new films, but when I added I would also like to screen once again *Ordet,* he was really scandalized: what, again this old Dreyer stuff? The same thing happens in Sweden when you ask for Bergman. For a long time they claimed his films were made only for foreigners. Don't forget that many German directors, Wenders is a typical example, left Germany because of the way they were treated there. I think the French are the only ones who really defend their national patrimony.

Q: *You have often talked in the past about the possibility of your adapting a literary work but until now it has never happened. All your screenplays are based on original scripts.*
A: I tried my hand at adaptations several times, but every single time, I gave up in the middle. It is difficult to adapt a book, certainly a book you love, without losing some of its original flavor and qualities. I can't think of a

successful adaptation of a great novel. I believe the best novels to turn into films are either thrillers or second-class literature. Orson Welles, for instance, took a rather routine crime story and made a masterpiece out of it in *Touch of Evil*. There are many more examples of this kind, for instance several of Godard's films. As for myself, right now I do not feel like doing a crime story, though I am still tempted by Malraux's *Human Condition*. But I realize that there will be always something missing in the transition to the screen.

Q : *It has been often said that each one of your films is a sequel of the previous one. Do you agree?*
A : It's true. This is the reason you will never find the word "End" at the end of any of my films. As far as I am concerned, these are chapters of one and the same film that goes on and will never be finished, for there is never a final word on anything. I believe we never manage to do more than a fraction of the things we'd like to do. My last film, *Eternity and a Day*, is attempting to convey the idea that a few words, acquired here and there, are never enough to complete a whole poem.

Q : *Your films seem to be very personal not only because your way of doing them is so different from all others, but also because they really talk about yourself, all through. One is often under the impression that your protagonist, even though an actor plays the part, is a reflection of yourself projected in a dramatic context quite close to certain aspects of your life. You even told me once that you seriously considered playing one of these parts, yourself.*
A : Yes, it is a bit like that. There are of course directors who play in their own films, like Orson Welles. Sometimes one cannot avoid the feeling, particularly when the film is very close to yourself, that no actor could do justice to the part. I felt like this in *Eternity and a Day*. In the early stages, I was uneasy with Bruno Ganz in the lead, but deep down it was my own identification with the part that generated my fear that no actor could fully satisfy my expectations. This is the reason that, at a certain point, I stopped the shoot. I needed to put myself at a certain distance from the script, put it in perspective and see the character wearing the features of another person. One could say the same things when discussing *Voyage to Cythera* or *Ulysses' Gaze*. The truth is that these characters are composite images. There is a smaller or greater part of yourself in each one of them, but there are also other persons you have known. It is never quite you but certainly some of

you is always there. And the deeper you go into those characters, the closer they are to your intimate self.

Q: *Another constant concern in your films is the father-son relationship.*
A: As I have told you before when we talked about my childhood, the father figure is very important in my own past. The absence of the father who has been taken away—and we had no idea whether he was still alive or not—has been a heavy load on all of us. Since my very first film, it was a crucially important point. *Reconstruction* opens with the return of the father. Later films deal with the search for the father figure, whether a real or a fictitious father, one who could be a point of reference for the entire film and its protagonist.

Q: *Another characteristic of your films—practically all of them are road movies.*
A: Yes, but with a difference. Usually, in road movies, the characters roam from one place to another without a definite purpose. In my films, these journeys always have a goal. In *Voyage to Cythera,* for instance, it is the journey to the imaginary island of one's dreams, the island of peace and happiness. In *Landscape in the Mist* the children are looking for their father. The reporter in *The Suspended Step of the Stork* is travelling around for a definite reason; he is trying to unveil the mystery of the politician who disappeared. In *Ulysses' Gaze* the entire trip through the Balkans is determined by the wish to find some pieces of lost film.

Q: *You said once that some films come from the heart, others from the mind. Is it true in your case?*
A: Some films have at their origins an intellectual premise. In others, it is sentiment. For instance, *The Hunters* was almost entirely conceived intellectually. The same for *Days of '36. The Beekeeper* comes straight from the heart. Most of my films are in-between, a combination of both.

Q: *There are, in your films, whether they come from the heart or the mind, magical moments that will stay with me forever. The party in* The Travelling Players, *the last shot of the old couple on the raft in* Voyage to Cythera, *the rape in* Landscape in the Mist, *the wedding in* The Suspended Step of the Stork, *the New Year party and Lenin's statue on the barge in* Ulysses' Gaze, *the bus ride in* Eternity and a Day. *And these are only a very few examples. Every time they occur, one is left amazed again and again by their originality, their imagination and poetry. Is it something that just happens while you're shooting the film or is it carefully prepared beforehand?*

A: Both. The bus ride was not at all written this way. Originally, in this scene, there were just the writer and the boy. It was an almost realistic scene, which could, of course, be very moving. Two persons in an empty bus, crossing the city in the rain. But somehow, I had the feeling it was not enough. This is why it took so long to shoot this scene. As we were shooting, I was gradually changing it. Finally, I did the scene twice, once following the script, a second time throwing the script away. The second version is the one we used. The scene of the party in *The Travelling Players,* when two men are dancing the tango together, had originally a few lines of dialog. Once we started rehearsing it, I decided to change it. The scene was taking place in 1946—people were still wearing at the time bowler hats, striped suits, and so on. At a certain moment, during a break in the rehearsal, I noticed two men, both wearing bowler hats, standing next to each other. The pianist was playing a few notes of a tango, one of them approached the other, and they started dancing together. That was completely unexpected. I had not written it in the script, not even thought of it, but that is how I rounded up this scene, and I believe it was the right way to do it. Sometimes, it's this kind of improvisation on the spot; sometimes you know what you're going to do a few days early. For the rape scene in *Landscape in the Mist,* it was like that. It was not in the script, but I had it already in mind several days before we shot it. As for the marriage scene in *The Suspended Step of the Stork* with the bride on one side of the river, the bridegroom on the other—when I wrote the script, the scene was different, but I felt something was missing there. Then, one day, I was in New York on a bus going to Bronx through Harlem. At a stop, I saw a small black boy improvising some dance steps on one side of the street, and on the other side, there was another small black boy, who was answering him with his own dance steps. Nothing out of the ordinary, maybe, but I immediately saw the river in the middle. And there is something else, something I read in 1958 about an island near Crete, a very small one, completely isolated in the winter. During those long months, the shepherds who live there use a sign language to communicate with a Cretan priest, who would watch for them at certain hours. They would inform him if someone was dead on their side, he would say mass in Crete for the deceased person, and they would bury the corpse on the small island. The combination of these two sources of inspiration resulted in the marriage as you see it in *The Suspended Step of the Stork*. The New Year party in *Ulysses' Gaze* was written more or less the way it is played. I knew it was all going to be in one shot, but I felt, when writing it, there was something missing, and as we were rehearsing, I added light touches here and there. As for the barge with Lenin's statue on it, this marks for me the end of an era. I had prepared the sequence beforehand, but the idea of having the peasants watching it float down the Danube and crossing themselves as it went by originated with something I saw in Constanza, a Romanian port on the Black Sea. A crane was moving a huge head of Lenin from a ship to a barge, when a fishing boat just happened by. The couple on it, a man and a woman, stood up, shocked, as if Lenin had just come back to life. The woman covered the man's eyes and instinctively made the sign of the cross.

But I have to say that strangely enough there are scenes you believe are crucial when you write the script, but do not seem at all like this once you have shot them. While other scenes, which you may not have been very keen on, turn out to be key moments in the film.

Q : *What is the role of music in your films?*
A : My relations with music in films have a long history. I started by refusing any type of background music; I accepted only music coming from natural sources. The folk song in *Reconstruction* was not background but an extension of the stones and the faces in that film. For me this kind of music is as essential to my films as the rain, for instance. The music in *The Days of '36* is limited to accidental broadcasts picked up on the radio. There is a lot more music in *The Travelling Players,* but those were songs performed by the actors in their show or to attract audiences to the show. I followed the same principle in *The Hunters,* and only in *Megalexandros* did I decide to change. Since the structure of the film is that of Byzantine liturgical music, I chose very old folk music played on antique instruments and used them in the liturgical tradition, alternating between solos and ensemble pieces. As a matter of fact, in this film I used two types of music—the Byzantine and that of the Italian anarchists who had their own songs. In a way, it is the juxtaposition of the Orient and the Occident. With Greece, of course, in the middle. In *Voyage to Cythera* I finally changed my approach, and since then, I've worked with Eleni Karaindrou on the soundtrack of all my subsequent films.

However, the music in my films has a very particular characteristic. It has a kind of obsessional quality, strictly related to a definite character. The protagonist in *Voyage to Cythera* wakes up in the morning and turns on his radio to listen to a piece of music. At the time I was particularly fond of Vivaldi's Concerto for Two Mandolins, which for me was the epitome of perfection. I played it for Eleni and told her I would like something similar to a concerto grosso, very much in the spirit of Vivaldi. She wrote it and that is what the character is listening to in the morning. Later, however, this same theme changes, turns into jazz, a popular song, a violin solo, takes on the specificity of the situations the character is going through. That is one of the musical themes. The second theme is related to the father, whose peasant origins come through in the music accompanying the scene in which he dances to honor the graves of the comrades he had left behind when he went away. The final piece of music combines the two themes together, that of the son and that of the father, in a kind of violin concerto, played as the old man and his wife drift away into the sea.

Q: *How precise are your indications to Eleni, when you work together on a soundtrack?*
A: We have a very close relationship. First I tell her the story of the next film. She has a tape recorder and records it. She does not want to read the script—she insists she needs to hear the sound of my voice and my inflections when telling the story. Strangely enough, I have the same request from all the actors in my films. It is not the scenario they want to familiarize themselves with, but my interpretation of it. It is probably because when I am telling a story, I do not do it in a logical, linear sequence. I am trying to create an adequate climate for it. The words I choose to express my thoughts, the structure of the phrases, the silences, all these establish a direct contact between me and my listeners, something they cannot get by reading a manuscript.

Q: *To go back to Eleni, does this mean she composes the music before the film is finished?*
A: Of course. She records my voice, goes home and listens to it, improvises on a synthesizer, and then we meet again. She sits at the piano and plays various themes. I listen, and when something catches my ear, I ask whether she can repeat the musical phrase she had just played but change it from major to minor, try a different rhythm, and so on. Once we find the key

phrase I need, in its right tonality, we are on the right track. In *Eternity and a Day*, for instance, I asked her not to write a sad piece, despite the fact that it might have seemed to be the obvious choice for a film dealing with a person who faces the distinct eventuality of death. In my eyes, however, the film is almost an invitation to life. Eleni had originally composed something very sad, probably because of her own state of mind, her father having died shortly before. But that was not at all what I was looking for. I told her what she had written was beautiful but not for me. She tried to insist, but I would not change my mind. And then she said she had a few more improvisations, which she didn't really find very interesting. She started playing and I immediately told her: "This is it." That was the key phrase for all the music of the film. Once we settle on the themes, I ask her for variations on specific instruments, on which we have to agree beforehand. The use of the accordion for *Ulysses' Gaze* was a specific request of mine. This instrument represents for me the musical climate of this part of the world. It is the instrument you hear during the trip of Lenin's statue down the Danube. Only once did Eleni choose something on her own, and I am still not quite sure whether she was right or not. It was the decision to use saxophonist Jan Garbarek for *The Beekeeper*. True enough, on this occasion it wasn't exactly jazz he was playing (though he does play plenty of jazz, with Keith Jarrett and others) but something much closer to Greek folk music. The soundtrack is something in between the two, not quite the one nor the other. I am satisfied with the music; however, I wonder whether there weren't other solutions, for there is still something that bothers me, the feeling that at times the music is not sufficiently integrated in the picture.

Q: *Eleni Karaindrou is one of your regular, faithful partners in filmmaking. Tonino Guerra, is another one. This is a strange relationship, him being an Italian who does not speak Greek, while you do not speak Italian. And yet, it is with him you start writing your scripts.*
A: It is true we do not need to speak the same language, but we are both men of the South. I believe that all the Mediterranean people have something in common. Not only because there are ancient roots common to all of us, having been in contact with each other for thousands of years, but also because of the proximity of the sea and the similitude of the climate. I never feel abroad when I am in Italy. With Tonino, it was an instant relationship. He was working at the time with Andrei Tarkovski in Rome on *Nostalghia*.

Andrei and I shared the same flat for a couple of weeks, a flat owned by an assistant director who worked with me on *Megalexandros* and with Tarkovski on *Nostalghia*. All I knew about Tonino at the time was his work with people like Fellini and Antonioni, but Andrei seemed to be very happy with their collaboration. I asked my assistant, the owner of the flat, to introduce us, and he arranged for me to go over to Tonino's place. I intended to meet him, get to know him, and then see whether there was a way for us to cooperate. Five minutes after I stepped into his flat, we were already at work. We immediately realized we were speaking the same language—in film terms of course, because when we met I spoke French and he spoke Italian but we understood each other perfectly. We also discovered there are many things for which we share the same affection and love. What I like about Tonino is not only the fact that he is a poet, but also that earthly, peasant side, which for me, is very important.

Q: *In practice, how do you proceed when you meet to work on a script?*
A: I must first explain that while basically, I am the author of my own scripts, I always need another person who will play the devil's advocate, the psychoanalyst or whatever, to give me a different perspective of the things I have in mind. He is to be the first person to hear my ideas in the raw, and his feedback helps me choose the right direction. In the case of Tonino, most of the time he acts the part of the psychoanalyst. I am not sure many people work together the way we do.

Once a film is finished and I feel I am ready to start the next one, I go to his village in the mountains. We sit down, talk about everything and anything, have a drink, and then go to lunch. Later, as we sit down and relax, he will ask me whether I have anything in mind I would like to work on. At this point I am still doubtful. I start talking, telling him different stories I had been reflecting upon, ideas that caught my fancy, images that stuck in my mind, nothing yet very organized one way or another. I am walking back and forth; he listens to me, sitting down. When there is something he considers to be of particular interest, he stops me and writes it down.

Q: *A bit like you and Eleni Karaindrou.*
A: Exactly. Later, we go through all the things he has noted, and we try to see whether there is a coherent idea in there. To do this, I take the notes, go to the room he has prepared for me, pore over them for a few hours, then

come back to the sitting room, and suggest a way to proceed. We go out, have a coffee, talk about the direction I proposed. He would tell me whether he likes it or not and add a few other related ideas he had in the afternoon while I was working in my room. Out of it comes another version, an improved one, of the same idea, and we go on like this for three, four days, discussing various options for the script. But we do not do it all the time, from morning till night. We eat, we go for long walks, we meet people in the village, and we also talk about the script. When I leave, I already have in mind a first draft. I call him and tell him about it, or I put it on paper and send him a copy. But he, too, prefers to hear me tell it, rather than read it. He gives me his opinion, and then I start working with a second person. Tonino assists at the birth of the original idea. And sometimes he can be quite insistent on certain details. For instance, he once called me in Greece after we had already completed the script for *Landscape in the Mist*, and he told me: "Listen Theo, we absolutely have to have a hen in the movie." "Where do you want me to put it?" I asked. "I don't know where," he replied, "but I feel we have to put a hen, somewhere." He was right and one of the scenes in the film opens with a hen.

The second person I work with is my first reader. In the past it was Thanassis Valtinos; these days it is Petros Markaris. Through him I get a first reaction to my script. Markaris, by the way, has written a whole book in which he describes our cooperation on *Eternity and a Day*. He never told me, but he documented everything we did, all our phone conversations, our discussions—he didn't leave anything out. Part of his job is to take the script I have written by hand and type it into a computer—I still can't use a typewriter, let alone a computer. He sends me this draft, and I put in my own corrections and additional remarks, and send it back to him. This goes on for some time, we either meet or exchange faxes of the drafts as they progress from one stage to the next, until I reach the point when I feel the others have given me everything they can, and I put in the last touches on my own. But the final shooting script you will find only if you take it off the finished print of the film. If you compare that with the script I have when I start shooting, you will find there are huge discrepancies between them.

Q: *The other person who has been working with you since the very beginning is your cameraman, Giorgos Arvanitis. How do you work together? After all, his is a very complicated, difficult job, given the kind of complex shots in your films.*

A: First of all, I have to mention that for the last three films, Arvanitis has done one half of the film and another cameraman, Andreas Sinanos, was in charge of the other half, and no one can tell their work apart. Not only because Sinanos has been the assistant of Arvanitis already on *Megalexandros* and he is therefore familiar with his work and, of course, with mine too. But also because I am always behind the cameraman, giving very precise instructions. Arvanitis, who has shot most of my films, knows me, naturally, very well. He is a rather difficult person to work with, not that I am that easy to get along with. Others who have worked with him didn't always have that good a time. With me, he is more compliant, not only because we've known each other for such a long time, but also because he likes my way of shooting, luckily, for ours is almost a kind of marriage. We've collaborated for some thirty-odd years. It's almost a lifetime. Most of the time, I don't have to tell him anything anymore. He knows exactly what to do and how to do it. With Sinanos, I am still checking every shot.

Q: *How do you explain what you want them to do? Do you draw the shots for them?*
A: No, I just tell them what I want and they understand. I have a very clear visual image of what I expect to see on the screen. Many years ago, I used to draw a storyboard for my assistant but now, having been with me for over twenty years, after studying in the class I used to teach at the Film School in Athens, he doesn't need my drawings anymore. He knows me well enough to guess immediately my intentions. After so many years together, none of them has any problem entering the particular universe of my films. It makes life very easy working with them, but there is a danger there, nonetheless. The risk of being tempted by the "deja vu."

Q: *Would you really consider, today, just to avoid this risk, changing your crew?*
A: Not really. After all, it is finally my responsibility, not theirs, to avoid the routine, to be aware of the risk I run by repeating myself. I am the only person who has a full, global image in my mind of everything the film should be, down to the smallest details, and I am the only one who can make any changes at all. But I would like to add one more thing. My set is run on the basis of what I would like to call "a controlled democracy." I discuss every scene with everybody who is there; I tell them exactly what I want to do and why I want to do it. I listen to all their comments, and sometimes I

use their suggestions, if I feel they are right. Arvanitis has contributed more than once ideas that not only facilitated the shooting itself but also supplied an additional dimension to a specific scene. By the way, there are a number of documentaries that followed the production of my films, showing the way I work with the crew.

Q: *I am not going to ask you about editing. The way you shoot your films, it should be elementary. But let's discuss, for a minute, your relation with the film itself. I know you entertain an almost physical relationship with the film. I remember your telling me how you check every print coming out of the lab. You were never very sympathetic to digital techniques, but lately, I heard you used this technique and the Avid system for some of your recent films.*

A: It's true that the images in my films are very easy to edit. The sound, on the other hand, is a very complicated issue. It is also true that in my recent films I used the Avid system, but in my next film, I am going back to the Moviola. I believe that every image you shoot for your film takes its toll on you. You invest something of yourself in it and to do it you need a very strong incentive. Unless there is a degree of satisfaction in your work, there is no use doing it. But with the digital system and Avid, there is no satisfaction for me. When I face a Moviola or an editing table, I feel the film. It is true I control every single print that goes out of the lab. I smell the emulsion with my nose, I touch it with my hands, I truly entertain a physical relationship with the film, and I am not the only one. I have seen several British films mentioning, at the end of their credits list, that they have been cut on an editing table. The same goes for the photography. Even if it is true that digital images can match or improve, today, on the quality of film, I still believe, and some people have already said it, that certain technical failures can help the picture. I recently read somewhere that Hollywood considers the possibility of introducing some flaws, intentionally, in their films, which have been far too smooth and perfect.

Q: *Let's talk about your actors. In your recent films you have again and again chosen non-Greek actors.*

A: Frankly, the nationality of the actors does not concern me at all. I want to have the best person for the part.

Q: *How about their not speaking Greek, the language in which you shoot all your films?*

A: I have often argued with many of my colleagues, for instance Bertolucci, about the importance of one's maternal language. For me, it is an inseparable part of our identity. These are the very first sounds you hear when you are born, and they should be an integral part of the films we make. This should not, however, become an insurmountable obstacle for there are ways of overcoming it. In *Ulysses' Gaze*, Keitel's character comes from America and therefore can speak English. Marcello Mastroianni learned Greek. For a whole week, once the shooting was over, I taught him phonetically every line he spoke in the film, before he went ahead and dubbed himself. I insisted on every inflection, on the diphthongs and the pronunciation of every single consonant that does not exist in Italian. He had asked to have his voice on the soundtrack, and he did it. True, it is an exception. Greek is a very difficult language to speak, certainly for someone who has never done it before. Possibly it is a bit easier for an Italian, because there is some kind of kinship in the sonority of the two languages. Keitel, who had to say a only few words in Greek, found it much more difficult. It was practically impossible to get him to say it right. For *Eternity and a Day* I had to have a Greek actor dub Bruno Ganz, and I wasn't very happy about it. I believe an actor's voice is part of his personality—without it he is not all there—and I felt badly to hear the voice of another actor coming from his mouth. It is well dubbed but it bothers me. On the other hand, I have to decide whether I am willing to give up the chance of working with certain actors who have marked my cinema life. Though, to be quite honest, I had never dreamed of working with Mastroianni or Jeanne Moreau.

With Mastroianni, it was a case of pure luck. For *The Beekeeper* I wanted Gian Maria Volonte. I already had him in mind for *Megalexandros* but it did not work out because his agent asked for the kind of money we simply did not have and I finally did the film with Omero Antonutti. But I still wanted to work with him. After finishing the script of *The Beekeeper*, Tonino Guerra asked me if I had already thought about an actor. I told him I wanted Volonte. "But he is very sick," he told me. At the time it was already common knowledge that Volonte had lung cancer and only one lung left. "Why don't you try Marcello Mastroianni?" "No, he is too handsome," I answered. "Let me call him," said Tonino, "he'll come over here and you can make up your mind." Twenty minutes later Marcello was there. I had never met him before. In my eyes he was a cinema icon, but he was someone who, so I thought, could only play either comic parts or in Fellini's *8½*. Certainly not the kind of person I needed for *The Beekeeper*. To convince him that he was wrong for the part, I set out to tell him the story of the film. But then, my own involvement carried me away. I was really going into details of the plot and looking at him. I noticed the expression on his face was changing in the most amazing way. at certain moments, I had the feeling his eyes were getting wet. I was almost speechless and realized he was the actor I was looking for. In his case I was right not only about his talent, but also about the person I discovered on the set. Marcello is the only foreign actor with whom I really worked. No need for preparations, no pussyfooting around, we were fully communicating from the very first shot on that film.

Q: *History and politics were once in the forefront of every film you made. Now, they are still there, very evident, but much more in the background. Not to mention the quote from* The Suspended of the Stork *which says: "Politics is nothing more than a career." You said earlier you were a man of the left; you certainly still are, but not in the same way.*

A: I think many things have changed around us through the years that have been making film. Already in *Megalexandros* I tried to portray a freedom fighter that turns into a tyrant. I felt that everything we believed in changes once it touches power. The film was a reflection on two themes, power and property. They corrupt all those who, to start with, may have been sincere idealistic socialists. I saw all around me the things that were happening under socialist regimes. I couldn't help noticing the changes taking place in all those people who were behind May '68. All the ideals we once had were being twisted and fading away. My first film to move history from the forefront to the background was *Voyage to Cythera*. It deals with people who believed once in historical perspective and political change, only to discover, thirty years after sacrificing practically everything they had for the revolution, that they are rejected by one and all. It is a political odyssey that ends with the old man, the hero who once dreamed of changing the world, and his wife, the only one who remained at his side, drifting out into the sea. You mentioned earlier the procession of Lenin's dismantled statue going down the Danube in *Ulysses' Gaze*. For me, this marks the end of a chapter in modern history. For many years, there was a strong belief the world could and should be changed for the better, and violent means were often used on both sides in the attempt to put down those who tried to bring about these changes. The nature of these changes became evident in those countries that lived for several decades under the communist regime. My generation was severely hurt by this violent conflict. We lived in Greece a civil war that left behind a country in ruins, both material and spiritual.

Q: *You seem to be very concerned about the future of the Balkans, literally a burning issue these days, when NATO is bombing Belgrade.*
A: I think we are reaching the end of pretty sad century. There were so many hopes and dreams when it started, hopes of a better world, more justice, better understanding between the peoples of the world. And when you look around today, you see more barriers and borders than ever, no mutual understanding whatsoever. On a technical level, communications have reached tremendous proportions. This should have made a great difference, but I am afraid it is only a fictitious notion. Real communication hardly exists at all.

Q: *In* The Suspended Step of the Stork *there is the officer who lifts his foot across the border and says that if he puts it down, he will die. So what would you consider a valid solution for him and for all of us? Abolish all borders?*
A: That was the real meaning of a united Europe, for me. The United States of Europe was our only hope to escape chauvinism and the hostility it breeds. Now it seems Europe is close to becoming one economic entity, but a united political entity seems very far away. And without it, it is very doubtful that an economic union can survive.

Q: *But do you really believe, knowing everything you know about human nature, there is any chance of seeing a world without borders?*
A: It's probably a utopia. However, maybe I am dreamer, but I am under the impression that only utopias can change the world and lead it forward.

Q: *Finally, let's discuss briefly the state of world cinema today. You once said that when you were young you used to see two, three films a day? Do you still see many films, nowadays?*
A: No. I don't have the time. It's a problem. Sometimes I still go to the cinema, but these are real events for which I pick the film very carefully beforehand. I have to confess I look from time to time at films on video, though I hate this way of viewing films. But I am doing it because I want to

keep in touch with the work of young people, some sent to me, others I pick out of interest and curiosity.

Q: *What I was trying to find out is your opinion of the cinema being made today. It seems that directors of your kind find themselves relegated to minor distributors and to art houses and all the rest is taken over by the big Hollywood machines.*
A: As far as I am concerned, I am still OK. Not only in Greece—here they still make quite a fuss over my films—but also in France and Germany, where they may not use hundreds of prints for my films but it is still a normal commercial distribution. In England, it's more or less the same. In Europe and some Asian countries, like Taiwan, Hong Kong, Japan or Israel, the distribution is still normal. But I do not know whether this situation will continue. I am not sure that I will not be relegated, once again, as I was at the very beginning, to art cinemas only. Let's face it, cinema changes very quickly. The main, and often the only, concern of the film industry now is the number of admissions for each film. It is to be expected, but it should not be its exclusive concern. People Like Welles and Dreyer, not to mention many others, have been marginals all their lives. But they were the ones to write the history of cinema. Personally, I believe that all the real changes, in whatever field you can think of, are not being made by the masses, but by a minority of people. The exceptional people.

Q: *But do you believe these exceptional people can find an outlet today?*
A: If not today, maybe tomorrow or the day after. I am not a pessimist, despite what many people may think. I am trying to see things as they are . . .

Q: *Some people may argue that you are a pessimist after all . . .*
A: No, I am not. I am a melancholic. And according to Aristotle, melancholia is the source of the creative spirit. I must also say I do not feel that all the record-breaking blockbusters succeeding each other should worry us overmuch. Some films may be tremendously successful but are soon forgotten; others are seen by only a few and yet they leave their mark on the history of cinema.

Q: *Have you seen any of this remarkable breed of films lately?*
A: I am afraid I haven't. But I trust that sooner or later they will emerge again.

Q: *But if they will ever come around, someone will have to be there and appreciate them. You have once been a film critic. Film critics have been instrumental in bringing your films to the audiences at large. What is your opinion of film criticism nowadays?*

A: I think it is a reflection of the media for which they work and the more I read it, the more I suspect it has very little to do with real criticism. The things they publish nowadays are mostly very superficial, impressionistic, without much thought or reflection behind them. Personally, I consider criticism should be as creative and as challenging as the work it refers to. It is not the case these days. I wouldn't like to generalize, but most critics are guided by the ratings as much as the films themselves. So what's the use of reading at all? In the past I would read a review written about one of my films, favorable or not, and discover, from time to time, certain things that even I did not realize before about them. Not any more. But hopefully, when the quality of the films improves, the critics will follow course.

Sometimes I have the feeling I am talking about my personal problems, maybe the problems of my generation. I see so many that have started at the same time I did and have given up in the meantime. Their cinema may have been quite different from mine, but we all sincerely tried to do something original, to give our audience the credit of being intelligent, to help them understand their own existence, to give them hope in a better future, to teach them how to dream again. Hopefully, it is not going to end here.

INDEX

Achilles, 69
Actors and acting, 30, 51, 60–62, 74, 92, 98–99, 114–15, 119, 135, 144–46
Aeschylus, 68
Agammemnon, 18, 20, 92
Albee, Edward, 67
Alexander the Great, 46, 68, 96
Andrieu, Michel, 129
Antonioni, Michelangelo, 13, 55, 61, 66, 67, 92, 111, 133, 141
Antonutti, Omero, 30, 145
Arcand, Denys, 58
Aristotle, 148
Arvanitis, Giorgos, 57, 142–44

Bach, Johann Sebastian, 126
Balkans, 83, 90, 91, 94, 96–97, 100, 115, 147
Balzac, Honoré de, 124
Beekeeper, The, 53–59, 60, 69, 70, 74, 81, 95, 114, 117, 118, 119, 136, 145, 146
Benedek, Laszlo, 71
Bergman, Ingmar, 68, 69, 75, 134; *The Seventh Seal*, 33
Bertolucci, Bernardo, 145
Black and White, 129
Borders, 78, 105–06, 107, 118
Borges, Jorge Luis, 112

Brecht, Bertolt, 12, 24, 25, 69, 131
Brogi, Giulio, 51

Cacoyannis, Michael: *Stella*, 71; *Never on Sunday*, 89; *Zorba the Greek*, 89
Cagney, James, 125
Calypso, 96
Camera, 23–24, 56–57, 86–87, 142–44
Camus, Albert, 126
Cannes Film Festival, 36, 80, 113, 122
Cavafy, Constantine, 52
Censorship, 8, 11
Chaplin, Charles "Charlie," 88, 95
Chekhov, Anton, 126
Chrysothemis, 20
Cinema, Greek, 6–7, 30–31, 71, 85, 134
Clitemnestra, 18, 19, 20
Curtiz, Michael, 84; *Angels with Dirty Faces*, 125

Dassin, Jules, 127
Dayan, Nissim, *A Very Narrow Bridge*, 77
Days of '36, 9–15, 17, 26, 29, 31, 38, 52, 66, 69, 81, 84, 87, 94, 131, 136, 138
Democratic Change (Demokratiki Allaghi), 132
Dos Passos, John, 67
Dostoyevski, Fyodor Mikhailovich, 126; *The Brothers Karamazov*, 126

Dovzhenko, Alexander, *Earth*, 33
Dreyer, Carl, 12, 148; *Ordet*, 130, 134; *The Passion of Jeanne d'Arc*, 13

Editing, 144
Egistus, 18, 19, 20
Eisenstein, Sergei, 72, 87, 130; *The Battleship Potemkin*, 75
Electra, 18, 19, 20
Emigration, 4, 43, 76–77
Eternity and a Day, 101–12, 113–16, 117–22, 135, 136, 142, 145
Euripides, 68

Father figure, 41, 54, 136
Faulkner, William, 67, 92
Fellini, Federico, 67, 91, 103, 134, 141; *8½*, 35, 145
Film distribution, 34–35, 38, 95–96
Film production, 5–6, 11, 30, 35–36, 101
Flynn, Errol, 127
Ford, John, 84, 88, 92
Frank, Cesar, 62
Freud, Sigmund, 48

Ganz, Bruno, 101, 102, 108, 115, 119, 135, 145
Gardner, Ava, 127
Gavras, Constantin, 13
Godard, Jean-Luc, 13, 63, 127, 135; *Breathless*, 67, 127
Goebbels, Josef, 9
Golfo, the Shepherdess, 20
Griffith, David W., 87
Guerra, Tonino, 63, 90, 93, 114, 140–42, 145
Gustafsson, Lars, 100

Hawks, Howard, 125
Hegel, Georg Wilhelm Friedrich, 48
Heidegger, Martin, 114, 121
Heller, Joseph, 67
Hemingway, Ernest, 67, 92
Heraklitos, 110
History, modern Greek, 3, 4, 5, 9–11, 12, 14– 15, 16–20, 29, 31, 36, 49–50, 53, 58, 70, 107, 125, 132
Hitchcock, Alfred, 63; *The Trouble with Harry*, 27
Homer, 68, 69; *The Odyssey*, 90, 93–94, 96
Hunters, The, 23–27, 30, 37, 38, 47, 56, 67, 69, 81, 87, 136, 138
Huston, John, 67, 125

Ibsen, Henrik, *Hedda Gabler*, 51
Ideologies, 37, 47–49, 69–70, 78, 79, 81–82, 97–98, 110–11, 146
IDHEC (Institut des Hautes Etudes Cinématographiques), 128, 132

Jancsó, Miklos, 31, 130
Josephson, Erland, 99

Karaindrou, Eleni, 138–40, 141
Karanghyosis (Greek puppet shows), 87
Karanovic, Srdjan, *Film with No Name*, 77
Karapiperis, Mikis, 57
Katrakis, Manos, 41, 51
Kazan, Elia, 127
Kazantzakis, Nicos, *The Odyssey: A Modern Sequel*, 88
Keitel, Harvey, 90, 91, 92, 98–99, 119, 145
Kelly, Gene, *Singing in the Rain*, 84
Kondouros, Nicos: *Drakos*, 71; *Paranomi*, 71
Kotamanidou, Eva, 30
Kubrick, Stanley, 130

Landscape in the Mist, 60–65, 69, 73, 74, 76, 77, 80, 81, 84, 85, 88, 105, 117, 119, 136, 137
Lang, Jacques, 96
Lenin, Vladimir Ilitch, 48, 97–98, 138, 146
Lester, Richard, 133
Locations, 3, 47, 55–56, 88, 95, 120, 133

Manaki, Yanaki and Milton, 90, 91, 94, 95, 98
Malraux, André, *Human Condition*, 135
Manzù, Giacomo, 91, 93
Markaris, Petros, 142

Markensinis, Spyros, 16
Marketaki, Tonia, 132
Marx, Karl, 48
Mastroianni, Marcelo, 53, 54, 58, 61, 62, 74, 77, 79, 83, 98, 109, 114, 119, 145, 146
Megalexandros, 28–32, 37, 46–47, 52, 54, 55, 69–70, 72, 73, 81, 86–87, 90, 117, 138, 141, 143, 145, 146
Mendelssohn, Felix, 62
Metaxas, Ioannis, 9–11, 14, 17, 125
Minelli, Vincente, 84
Mizoguchi, Kenji, 32, 66, 92; *Ugetsu Monogatari*, 130
Moreau, Jeanne, 145
Mozart, Wolfgang Amadeus, 126
Murnau, Friedrich, 31, 92; *The Last Laugh*, 130; *Sunrise*, 130
Music, 40, 44, 62–63, 126, 138–40
Mussolini, Benito, 9, 14, 79
Mythology, Greek, 17–20, 28, 46, 70, 90, 94, 96

Nichols, Mike: *Catch-22*, 67; *The Day of the Dolphin*, 67; *Who's Afraid of Virginia Woolf*, 67

Odysseus (Ulysses), 46, 58, 69, 88, 91, 93, 94
Oedipus, 30
Onassis, Aristotle, 15
Orestes, 18, 61, 63
Oshima, Nagisa, 65, 70; *The Ceremony*, 13; *Death by Hanging*, 13
Ozu, Yasujiro, 92

Palaiologlou, Tania, 61, 85
Papadopoulos, Giorgos, 16
Papagos, Alexandros, 17
Pasolini, Pier Paolo, 111
Penelope, 46, 93
Personal history, 39, 64, 117, 123–25, 126–29, 132–33
Philip the Second (father of Alexander the Great), 96

Philipopoulis. *See* Plovdiv
Pindar, 14
Plovdiv (Philipopoulis), 96
Polonski, Abraham, 125
Power, Tyrone, 127
Preferences and references, 13, 31, 32, 67–68, 84, 88, 125–26, 130, 147–84
Pylade, 18

Reconstruction, 3–8, 38, 70, 82, 84, 86, 92, 123, 124, 131, 136, 138
Reggiani, Serge, 53, 58
Renoir, Jean, 130, 134
Resnais, Alain, 127
Rosi, Francesco, 13, 58
Rouch, Jean, 129, 132

Sadoul, Georges, 127
Sartre, Jean Paul, 126
Scorsese, Martin, *GoodFellas*, 114
Script writing, 18, 23, 42, 48, 74, 84, 103–04, 140–42
Semprun, Jorge, *To Live or to Write*, 116
Sequence shot, 21–22, 25–26, 31–32, 64, 71–73, 87, 90, 92, 114
Seferis, George, 43, 52
Sinanos, Andreas, 143
Skevis, Achilles, 119
Solomos, Dyonisios, 107, 120–21
Sophocles, 68
Sound, 24, 62–63
Steinbeck, John, 67
Stendhal (Marie-Henri Beyle), *La Chartreuse de Parme, Le Rouge et le Noir*, 126
Straub, Jean-Marie, *Othon*, 13
Suspended Step of the Stork, 75–82, 83–88, 95, 100, 109, 114, 117, 136, 137, 138, 146, 147
Synchronos Kinematographos (film publication), 12

Tarantino, Quentin, 90
Tarkovsky, Andrei, 35, 66, 85, 140–41; *Nostalghia*, 64, 140; *Sacrifice*, 64; *Stalker*, 64

Taviani, Paolo and Vittorio, 58, 70; *Padre Padrone*, 30
Telemachus, 46
Television, 75–76, 95
Theodorakis, Mikis, 44
Thessaloniki Film Festival, 11, 31
Thomson, David, 113
Tolstoi, Leo, 126
Travelling Players, 16–22, 23, 24, 25, 26, 27, 28, 29, 30, 35, 38, 40, 55, 56, 59, 67, 69, 71, 73, 74, 79, 81, 84, 85, 86, 87, 89, 103, 104, 113, 134, 136, 137, 138
Trintignant, Jean-Louis, 115
Truffaut, François, 105
Tsitsanis, Vassilis, 44
Tzortzoglou, Stratos, 61

Ulysses. *See* Odysseus
Ulysses' Gaze, 89–92, 93–100, 113, 114, 117, 119, 122, 129, 130, 135, 136, 138, 145, 146

Valtinos, Thanassis, 142
Vangelis (composer), *Chariots of Fire*, 133
Visconti, Luchino, 67; *Ossessione*, 3
Vivaldi, Antonio, 40, 126, 139
Volonte, Gian-Maria, 114, 145
Voyage to Cythera, 33–38, 39–52, 53, 54, 58, 59, 64, 69, 74, 81, 82, 84, 88, 94, 117, 125, 135, 136, 138, 139, 146

Walsh, Raoul, 125
Welles, Orson, 32, 130, 135, 148; *The Magnificent Ambersons*, 130; *A Touch of Evil*, 89, 130, 135
Wenders, Wim, 115, 133, 134; *Alice in the Cities*, 61; *Paris, Texas*, 42; *Wings of Desire*, 61
Whitman, Walt, 67

Zeke, Michalis, 61
Zweig, Stefan, 124

www.ingramcontent.com/pod-product-compliance
Lightning Source LLC
Chambersburg PA
CBHW021842220426
43663CB00005B/369